The Numinous Way of Pathei-Mathos

David Myatt

θάνατος δὲ τότ᾽ ἔσσεται ὁππότε κεν δὴ Μοῖραι ἐπικλώσωσ᾽

Fifth Edition
2018

Contents

Prefatory Note

The numinous way - the philosophy - of pathei-mathos (πάθει μάθος) represents my weltanschauung, and which philosophy I advanced after I had, upon reflexion, rejected much of and revised what then remained of the 'numinous way', and which 'numinous way' I developed between 2006 and 2011.

Included here are all of my writings concerning this philosophy, penned in 2012; a slightly revised version of an older (2011) essay, *The Abstraction of Change as Opposites and Dialectic*, which has some relevance to that philosophy; and an appendix concerning my use of words such as Δίκα, σωφρονεῖν, and physis.

The Conspectus summarizes the philosophy of pathei-mathos, and, as the title might suggest, in a few places paraphrases, or utilizes, short passages from some of the other writings included here.

For this fifth edition, I have included five new appendices in order to elucidate terms such as 'numinous' and 'physis', added some other terms to the Glossary, and corrected some typos.

David Myatt
2018

○ ○ ○

θάνατος δὲ τότ᾽ ἔσσεται ὁππότε κεν δὴ Μοῖραι ἐπικλώσωσ᾽

"Our ending arrives whenever wherever the Moirai decide."
Attributed to Καλλίνου, as recorded by Ἰωάννης Στοβαῖος in Ἀνθολόγιον (c. 5th century CE)

Part One

Conspectus of The Philosophy of Pathei-Mathos

I. Morality, Virtues, and Way of Life
II. Wisdom, Pathei-Mathos, and Humility
III. Enantiodromia and The Separation-of-Otherness

I. Morality, Virtues, and Way of Life

For the philosophy of Pathei-Mathos, 'the good' is considered to be what is fair; what alleviates or does not cause suffering; what is compassionate; what is honourable; what is reasoned and balanced. This knowing of the good arises from the (currently underused and undeveloped) natural human faculty of empathy, and which empathic knowing is different from, supplementary and complimentary to, that knowing which may be acquired by means of the Aristotelian essentials of conventional philosophy and experimental science.

Empathy thus inclines a person toward certain virtues; toward a particular type of personal character; and disinclines them toward doing what is bad, what is unfair; what is harsh and unfeeling; what intentionally causes or contributes to suffering.

For empathy enables us to directly perceive, to sense, the φύσις (the physis, qv. Appendix IV) of human beings and other living beings, involving as empathy does a translocation of ourselves and thus a knowing-of another living-being as that living-being is, without presumptions and sans all ideations, all projections, all assumed or believed categories or categorizations. For empathy involves a numinous sympathy with another living-being; a becoming – for a causal moment or moments – of that other-being, so that we know, can feel, can understand, the suffering or the joy of that living-being. In such moments, there is no distinction made between them and us – there is only the flow of life; only the presencing and the ultimate unity of Life, of ψυχή, with our individuals self understood as just one fallible, fragile, microcosmic, mortal emanation of Life, and which emanation can affect other life in a good way or a bad way. In addition, empathy and pathei-mathos, provide us with the understanding that we human beings have the ability - the character - (or can develop the ability, the character) to understand and to restrain ourselves, to decide to do what is good and not do what is wrong. This ability of reason, this choice, and this ability to develope our character, are the genesis of culture and express our natural potential as human beings.

The numinous sympathy - συμπάθεια (sympatheia, benignity) - with another living being that empathy provides naturally inclines us to treat other living beings as we ourselves would wish to be treated: with fairness, compassion, honour, and dignity. It also inclines us not to judge those whom we do not know; those beyond the purveu - beyond the range of - our faculty of empathy. There is thus or there developes or there can develope:

(i) Wu-wei, the cultivation of an inner balance arising from an appreciation of the natural change (the flux) of living beings and how it is unbalanced, and harsh, of us to interfere in ways which conflict with the natural character of such beings and with that natural change. Part of this appreciation is of the numinous; another is of our own limits and limitations because we ourselves are only a small part of such natural change, an aspect of which is Nature; and which appreciation of the numinous and of our limits incline us toward a certain humility.

(ii) An appreciation of innocence, for innocence is regarded as an attribute of those who, being personally unknown to us, are therefore unjudged by us and who thus are given the benefit of the doubt. For this presumption of innocence of others – until direct personal experience, and individual and empathic knowing of them, prove otherwise – is the fair, the reasoned, the numinous, the human and cultured, thing to do.

(iii) An appreciation of how and why a personal and loyal love between two individuals is the most beautiful, the most numinously human, thing of all.

Thus among the virtues of the philosophy - the way - of pathei-mathos are compassion; self-restraint [εὐταξία], fairness, honour; manners; wu-wei, and a reasoned personal judgement.

Living according to the way of pathei-mathos therefore simply means:
- being compassionate or inclining toward compassion by trying to avoid causing, or contributing, to suffering;
- being honourable - fair, reasonable, well-mannered, just, dignified, tolerant, balanced;
- appreciating the value and importance of personal love;
- inclining toward a personal humility;
- appreciating the numinous;
- cultivating empathy and wu-wei.

In essence, The Way of Pathei-Mathos is an ethical, an interior, a personal, a non-political, a non-interfering, a non-religious but spiritual, way of individual reflexion, individual change, and empathic living, where there is an awareness of the importance of virtues such as compassion, humility, tolerance, gentleness, and love.

II. Wisdom, Pathei-Mathos, and Humility

Over millennia, the accumulated pathei-mathos of individuals - often evident in Art, literature, memoirs, music, myths, legends, and often manifest in the ethos of a religious-type awareness or in spiritual allegories – has produced certain insights, certain intimations of wisdom, one of which was the need for a balance, for ἁρμονίη, achieved by not going beyond the numinous limits; an intimation evident in Taoism, and in Greek myths and legends where this unwise 'going beyond' is termed ὕβρις - hubris - and well-described by, for example, Sophocles in Antigone and Oedipus Tyrannus.

Another intimation of wisdom - and perhaps one of the most significant - is pathei-mathos, with Aeschylus writing, in his Agamemnon, that the Immortal, Zeus, guiding mortals to reason, provided we mortals with a new law, which law replaces previous ones, and which new law – this new guidance laid down for mortals – is pathei-mathos. That is, that for we human beings, pathei-mathos possesses a numinous, a living, authority; that the wisdom, the understanding, that arises from one's own personal experience, from formative experiences that involve some hardship, some grief, some personal suffering, is often or could be more valuable to us (more alive, more meaningful) than any doctrine, than any religious faith, than any words one might hear from someone else or read in some book.

Pathei-mathos thus, like empathy, offers a certain understanding, a knowing; and, when combined, pathei-mathos and empathy are or can be a guide to wisdom, to a particular conscious knowledge concerning our own nature, our relation to Nature, and our relation to other human beings. Or, expressed philosophically, they can reveal the nature of Being and beings.

Since the range of our faculty of empathy is limited to the immediacy-of-the-moment and to personal interactions, and since the learning wrought by pathei-mathos and pathei-mathos itself is and are direct and personal, then the knowledge, the understanding, that empathy and pathei-mathos reveal and provide is of the empathic scale of things and of our limitations of personal knowing and personal understanding. That is, what is so revealed is not some grand or grandiose theory or praxis or philosophy which is considered applicable to others, or which it is believed can or should be developed to be applicable to others or developed to offer guidance beyond the individual in political and/or social and/or religious and/or ideological terms; but rather a very personal, individual, spiritual and thus interior, way. A way of tolerance and humility, where there is an acceptance of the unwisdom, the hubris, the unbalance, of arrogantly, pejoratively, making assumptions about who and what are beyond the range of our empathy and outside of our personal experience. That is, we are honest we do not know when we do not know; we accept that we do not have enough knowledge and/or experience to form and express an opinion about matters we have not studied and have no personal experience of, and about people we do not know and have not personally interacted with over a period of time. We accept that our empathy and pathei-mathos - our personal judgement, our experience, our interior appreciation of the numinous, the knowledge personally acquired - are what inform and guide us: not faith and not the rhetoric or the words or the passion or the propaganda or the ideas or the dogma or the policies or the ideology of others.

There is therefore an appreciation, a knowing, that is the genesis of a balanced and personal judgement - a discernment – and which knowing is evidential of our perception of Being and beings. Which is of how all living beings are emanations of Being, of ψυχή, and of how the way of non-suffering-causing moral change and reform both personal and social is the way of individual, interior, change; of aiding, helping, assisting other individuals in a direct, a personal manner, and in practical ways, because our perception is that of the human scale of things; of ourselves as fallible, and of individuals as individuals, as fellow human beings presumed innocent and good, or capable of reforming change, until direct experience and knowledge of them reveals otherwise.

III. Enantiodromia and The Separation-of-Otherness

The revealing concerning our own nature, our relation to Nature, and our relation to other human beings, that empathy and pathei-mathos provide is, as mentioned previously, of how all living beings are emanations of ψυχή, and thus of what is beyond 'the separation-of-otherness' that our division (instinctive or otherwise) into our self and the others causes. A revealing that this 'separation-of-otherness' is mere causal appearance, and which appearance not only obscures the nature of Being and of beings, but is also the genesis of hubris, and thence of suffering; a path away from wisdom.

Part of this 'separation-of-otherness' is when we (again, instinctively or otherwise) divide people into assumed categories and thus assign to them some term or some label or some name. We then presume we 'know' them as we often then prejudge them on the basis of the qualities (or lack of them) we or others have assigned to or associate with that category or term or label or name. In addition, we often or mostly come to define ourselves - provide ourselves with identity and our life with meaning - by accepting or assuming or assigning ourselves (or allowing others to so assign us) to a human manufactured category or categories. However, all these categories, terms, labels, names - and the duties and responsibilities, and/or likes/dislikes, assigned to them - have been and are the genesis of suffering, for they lead to and have led to certain categories being regarded as 'better than', or opposed to, others, and from notions of superiority/inferiority, of liked/hated opposites/enemies, conflict arises; both personal conflict, and the supra-personal conflict of some human beings, assigned to or identifying with some category, fighting/killing/hating /subjugating some other human beings assigned to or identifying with some other category.

For millennia, the periodicity of such assigning to, such identification with, such conflict between, human manufactured categories has continued. Old categories fade away, or are renamed, or become extinct; new ones are manufactured. Sometimes, categories become merged, forming a new type, assigned a new name. And the suffering, the lack of understanding about the nature of Being and beings, 'the separation-of-otherness', continues.

Enantiodromia is the term used, in the philosophy of pathei-mathos, to describe the revealing, the process, of perceiving, feeling, knowing, beyond causal appearance and the separation-of-otherness and thus when what has become separated – or has been incorrectly perceived as separated – returns to the wholeness, the unity, from whence it came forth. When, that is, beings are understood in their correct relation to Being, beyond the causal abstraction of different/conflicting ideated opposites, and when as a result, a reformation of the individual, occurs. A relation, an appreciation of the numinous, that empathy and pathei-mathos provide, and which relation and which appreciation the accumulated pathei-mathos of individuals over millennia have made us aware of or tried to inform us or teach us about.

For all living religions, all living spiritual ways, manifest or have expressed or were founded to express this same wisdom. Christianity, Islam, Judaism, Hinduism, Sikhism, Buddhism, Taoism, all - in their own particular way and beyond their different outer manifestations and the different terms and expressions and allegories used to elucidate 'that of the numinous' - express, enhance (or can enhance), our humanity: our ability to restrain ourselves, to admit our unknowing, to admit our mistakes, to perceive beyond our self and beyond 'the separation-of-otherness'. To be compassionate, forgiving, and receptive to humility and reformation.

Enantiodromia is therefore nothing new, accept that the process, the discovery, the reformation, is - in the philosophy of pathei-mathos - a natural one that does not involve any theory, or dogma, or praxis, or require any faith or belief of any kind. Rather, there is the personal cultivation of empathy, of wu-wei, an appreciation of the numinous, and the personal knowledge discovered by pathei-mathos; and that is all.

Part Two

The Way of Pathei-Mathos

A Philosophical Compendiary

- Introduction
- I - Pathei-Mathos as Authority and Way
- II - The Nature and Knowledge of Empathy
- III - The Nature of Being and of Beings
- IV - An Appreciation of The Numinous
- Conclusion

Introduction

The philosophy of πάθει μάθος (pathei-mathos) may be said to represent both the essence and the substance of what I have retained after refining and reflecting upon 'the numinous way' I developed between the years 2006 and 2011.

This year-long process of refinement and reflexion [2011-2012] led me to not only discard most of that 'numinous way' but also to re-express, in a more philosophical manner, the basic insights and the personal pathei-mathos that initially inspired me to develope that 'numinous way', a re-expression contained in this 'way of pathei-mathos' essay and in the following three essays: (1) Some

Personal Musings On Empathy; (2) Enantiodromia and The Reformation of The Individual; (3) Society, Politics, Social Reform, and Pathei-Mathos. These four essays should also serve to distinguish my new philosophy from that old 'numinous way'.

The philosophy of πάθει μάθος, however, is not a conventional, an academic, one where a person intellectually posits or constructs a coherent theory - involving ontology, epistemology, ethics, and so on - often as a result of an extensive dispassionate study, review, or a criticism of the philosophies or views, past and present, advanced by other individuals involved in the pursuit of philosophy as an academic discipline or otherwise. Instead, the philosophy of pathei-mathos is the result of my own pathei-mathos, my own learning from diverse - sometimes outré, sometimes radical and often practical - ways of life and experiences over some four decades; of my subsequent reasoned analysis, over a period of several years, of those ways and those experiences; of certain personal intuitions, spread over several decades, regarding the numinous; of an interior process of personal and moral reflexion, lasting several years and deriving from a personal tragedy; and of my life-long study and appreciation of Hellenic culture, an appreciation that led me to translate works by Sappho, Sophocles, Aeschylus and Homer, and involved me in a detailed consideration of the weltanschauung of individuals such as Heraclitus (insofar as such weltanschauungen are known from recorded sayings and surviving books).

Given this appreciation, and as the name suggests, the philosophy of πάθει μάθος has certain connexions to Hellenic culture and I tend therefore to use certain Greek words in order to try and elucidate my meaning and/or to express certain philosophical principles regarded as important in - and for an understanding of - this philosophy; a usage of words which I have endeavoured to explain as and where necessary, sometimes by quoting passages from Hellenic literature or other works and by providing translations of such passages. For it would be correct to assume that the ethos of this philosophy is somewhat indebted to and yet - and importantly - is also a development of the ethos of Hellenic culture; an indebtedness obvious in notions such as δίκη, πάθει μάθος, avoidance of ὕβρις, and references to Heraclitus, Aeschylus, and others, and a development manifest in notions such as empathy and the importance attached to the virtue of compassion.

In addition, and possibly somewhat unconventionally since in accord with the Hellenic etymology of the word and the Homeric sense of φίλος [a] I view a philosopher as someone who is a friend of – whose companion is, who seeks to find, to acquire, to follow, to befriend – σοφόν. Thus in this sense, a philosopher is someone seeking to acquire a certain skill (such as the learning/reasoning that is λόγος) and discover a particular knowledge, such as a knowledge regarding Being and beings, rerum divinarum et humanarum; a knowledge acquired or found by means of both using λόγος and from life itself via practical experience, practical learning; a dual sense evident from the meaning and usage of σοφός.

Thus my personal understanding of philosophy is that it is the result of the activity and the life of a philosopher; more correctly perhaps, it is both the written or the recorded or transmitted results of the lucubrations that such way of life (that such a following, such a seeking, of knowledge and wisdom) engenders, and of what the living of such a life (that such befriending of σοφόν) brings-into-being and/or reveals. And it is in this sense that I consider my way of πάθει μάθος a philosophy.

All translations from Ancient Greek in this work are mine, and I have, at the suggestion of a friend, added a Glossary giving some brief explanations and definitions of some of the Greek and English terms used.

[a] For example, Odyssey, Book I, v.301-302

καὶ σύ, φίλος, μάλα γάρ σ᾽ ὁρόω καλόν τε μέγαν τε,
ἄλκιμος ἔσσ᾽, ἵνα τίς σε καὶ ὀψιγόνων ἐὺ εἴπῃ.

Thus should you, my friend - who I see are strong and fully-grown -
Be as brave, so that those born after you will speak well of you.

I
Pathei-Mathos as Authority and Way

The Greek term πάθει μάθος derives from The Agamemnon of Aeschylus (written c. 458 BCE), and can be interpreted, or translated, as meaning learning from adversary, or wisdom arises from (personal) suffering; or personal experience is the genesis of true learning.

However, this expression should be understood in context [1], for what Aeschylus writes is that the Immortal, Zeus, guiding mortals to reason, has provided we mortals with a new law, which law replaces previous ones, and which new law – this new guidance laid down for mortals – is pathei-mathos.

Thus, for we human beings, pathei-mathos possesses a numinous, a living, authority [2] – that is, the wisdom, the understanding, that arises from one's own personal experience, from formative experiences that involve some hardship, some grief, some personal suffering, is often or could be more valuable to us (more alive, more meaningful) than any doctrine, than any religious faith, than any words one might hear from someone else or read in some book.

In many ways, this Aeschylean view is an enlightened – a very human – one, and is somewhat in contrast to the faith and revelation-centred view of religions such as Judaism, Islam, and Christianity. In the former, it is the personal experience of learning from, and dealing with, personal suffering and adversity, that is paramount and which possesses authority and 'meaning'. In the latter, it is faith that some written or transmitted work or works is or are a sacred revelation from the supreme deity one believes in which is paramount, which possess meaning and authority, often combined with a belief that this supreme deity has appointed or authorized some mortal being or beings, or some Institution, as their earthly representative(s), and which Institution and/or representative(s) therefore are believed to possess or are accepted as possessing authority or are regarded as authoritative.

Thus, the Aeschylean view is that learning, and hence wisdom, often or perhaps mostly arises from within us, by virtue of that which afflicts us (and which afflictions could well be understood as from the gods/Nature or from some supra-personal source) and from our own, direct, personal, practical, experience. In contrast, the conventional religious view is that wisdom can be found in some book (especially in some religious text), or be learnt from someone considered to be an authority, or who has been appointed as some authority by some Institution, religious or otherwise.

The essential difference between these two ways is therefore that pathei-mathos is the way of direct learning from personal experience, while the religious way is often or mostly the way of secondary or tertiary learning, from others; of accepting or believing what is written by or taught by someone else or laid down in some dogma, some creed, some book, or by some external authority, such as an Institution.

For The Way of Pathei-Mathos, it is the personal learning that pathei-mathos provides or can provide, combined with - balanced by - the insight, the knowing, that empathy provides, which are considered as possessing authority, and which can aid us to discover wisdom.

The Way of Pathei-Mathos

The fundamental axioms of The Way of Pathei-Mathos are:

1) That human beings possess a mostly latent perceptive faculty, the faculty of empathy - ἐμπάθεια - which when used, or when developed and used, can provide us with a particular type of knowing, a particular type of knowledge, and especially a certain knowledge concerning the φύσις (the physis, the nature or character) of human beings and other living beings.

2) This type of knowing, this perception, is different from and supplementary to that acquired by means of the Aristotelian essentials of conventional philosophy and experimental science [3], and thus enables us to better understand Phainómenon, ourselves, and other living beings.

3) That because of or following πάθει μάθος there is or there can be a change in, a development of, the nature, the character - the φύσις - of the person because of that revealing and that appreciation (or re-appreciation) of the numinous whose genesis is this πάθει μάθος, and which appreciation of the numinous includes an awareness of why ὕβρις is an error (often the error) of unbalance, of disrespect or ignorance (of the numinous), of a going beyond the due limits, and which ὕβρις itself is the genesis both of the τύραννος [4] and of the modern error of extremism. For the tyrannos and the modern extremist (and their extremisms) embody and give rise to and perpetuate ἔρις [5] and thus are a cause of, or contribute to and aid, suffering.

4) This change, this development of the individual, is or can be the result of enantiodromia [6] and reveals the nature of, and restores in individuals, the natural balance necessary for ψυχή [7] to flourish - which natural balance is δίκη as Δίκα [8] and which restoration of balance within the individual results in ἁρμονίη [9], manifest as ἁρμονίη (harmony) is in the cultivation, in the individual, of wu-wei [10] and σωφρονεῖν (a fair and balanced personal, individual, judgement) [11].

5) The development and use of empathy, the cultivation of wu-wei and σωφρονεῖν, are thus a means, a way, whereby individuals can cease to cause suffering or cease to contribute to, or cease to aid, suffering.

6) The reason as to why an individual might so seek to avoid causing suffering is the reason, the knowledge - the appreciation of the numinous - that empathy and πάθει μάθος provide.

7) This appreciation of the numinous inclines or can incline an individual to living in a certain way and which way of life naturally inclines the individual toward developing, in a natural way - sans any methodology, praxis, theory, dogma, or faith - certain attributes of character, and which attributes of character include compassion, self-restraint, fairness, and a reasoned, a personal, judgement.

II
The Nature and Knowledge of Empathy

Empathy is, as an intuitive understanding, what was, can be, and often is, learned or developed by πάθει μάθος. That is, from and by a direct, personal, learning from experience and suffering. An understanding manifest in our awareness of the numinous and thus in the distinction we have made, we make, or we are capable of making, between the sacred and the profane; the distinction made, for example in the past, between θεοί and δαιμόνων and mortals, and thus manifest in that understanding of ὕβρις and δίκη which can be obtained from the works of Sophocles, and Aeschylus [12], and from an understanding of Φύσις evident in some of the sayings attributed to Heraclitus [13].

Understood by reference to such classical illustrations, empathy is thus what naturally predisposed us to appreciate δίκη and be aware, respectful of, the goddess, Δίκην [14], and thus avoid retribution for committing the error of ὕβρις, for disrupting the natural balance necessary for individual and communal well-being.

That is, a certain empathy is, and has been, the natural basis for a tradition which informs us, and reminds us - through Art, literature, myths, legends, the accumulated πάθει μάθος of individuals, and often through a religious-type awareness - of the need for a balance, for ἁρμονίη, achieved by not going beyond the numinous limits.

As a used and a developed faculty, the perception that empathy provides is of undivided ψυχή and of the emanations of ψυχή, of our place in the Cosmic Perspective: of how we are a connexion to other life; of how we are but one mortal fallible emanation of Life; of how we affect or can affect the well-being - the very being, ψυχή - of other mortals and other life; and how other mortals and other living beings interact with us and can affect us, in a good or a harmful way.

Empathy thus involves a translocation of ourselves and thus a knowing-of another living-being as that living-being is, without presumptions and sans all ideations, all projections. In a simple way, empathy involves a numinous sympathy with another living-being; a becoming – for a causal moment or moments – of that other-being, so that we know, can feel, can understand, the suffering or the joy of that living-being. In such moments, there is no distinction made between them and us – there is only the flow of life; only the presencing and the ultimate unity of Life itself.

This knowing-of another living-being and this knowledge of the Cosmic Perspective - this empathic awareness of Life - inclines us toward compassion; toward the human virtue of having συμπάθεια (sympatheia, benignity) with and toward other living beings. For such an awareness involves being sensitive to, respectful of, other Life, and not arrogantly, in a hubriatic manner, imposing ourselves or trying to impose ourselves on Life and its emanations. That is, there is the cultivation of the natural balance that is wu-wei because of our awareness of how other Life, other living-beings, can suffer, and how some-things, some actions, are unwise because they do or can cause suffering or have caused suffering.

In effect, empathy uncovers or can uncover the nature of our being and the nature of Being itself.

III
The Nature of Being and of Beings

Empathy uncovers the a-causal nature of Being; of how, as Heraclitus expressed it in fragment 53, beings have their genesis,

> Πόλεμος πάντων μὲν πατήρ ἐστι, πάντων δὲ βασιλεύς, καὶ τοὺς μὲν θεοὺς ἔδειξε τοὺς δὲ ἀνθρώπους, τοὺς μὲν δούλους ἐποίησε τοὺς δὲ ἐλευθέρους.
>
> Polemos our genesis, governing us all to bring forth some gods, some mortal beings with some unfettered yet others kept bound. [15]

and how

> πάντα δὲ γίνεσθαι καθ᾽ εἱμαρμένην καὶ διὰ τῆς ἐναντιοδρομίας ἡρμόσθαι τὰ ὄντα
>
> All by genesis is appropriately apportioned [separated into portions] with beings bound together again by enantiodromia [16]

and why σωφρονεῖν is important:

σωφρονεῖν ἀρετὴ μεγίστη, καὶ σοφίη ἀληθέα λέγειν καὶ ποιεῖν κατὰ φύσιν ἐπαίοντας

Most excellent is balanced reasoning, for that skill can tell inner character from outer. [17]

Empathy also reveals why the assumption that abstracted, ideated, opposites apply to or should apply to living beings - and that they thus can supply us with knowledge and understanding of living being - disrupts the natural balance, resulting in a loss of ἁρμονίη and συμπάθεια and is therefore a manifestation of the error of ὕβρις.

The Acausal Nature of Being

The empathic perception of an undivided ψυχή and of living beings as emanations of ψυχή, and the knowledge of ourselves and one affective and effecting fallible mortal connexion to other life that such a perception provides, leads to an understanding of Being, of ψυχή, as a-causal: as beyond the linearity of a simple and direct cause-and-effect and beyond the supposition that we are separated beings. This perception - and this knowing of the acausal nature of Being deriving from it - is numinous; that is, of how beings are part of Being and of how they come-into-being, are affected and affecting, and so Change and are Change: of how Life flows and ebbs and continues undivided, unseparated, a-temporal, and is only temporarily manifest in particular beings only erroneously perceived by us as discrete entities, as separated beings.

As Heraclitus mentioned as recorded in fragment 52:

αἰὼν παῖς ἐστι παίζων πεσσεύων· παιδὸς ἡ βασιληίη

For Aeon, we are a game, pieces moved on some board: since, in this world of ours, we are but children.

For the perception and the knowing of causality in respect of living beings is that of the-separation-of-otherness; a notion of causal and linear separation, of past-present-future, of independent beings that gives rise to two things. (1) Of how we human consider we are different from or similar to other individual human beings. A difference or a similarity deriving from posited, manufactured, ideated, categories to which we assign others and ourselves and from which we often or mostly derive our identity, our self-assurance, and our belief about their and our φύσις, or at least what we assume is a knowledge of such things. (2) Of how such separately existing human beings are not subject to - or can and should make themselves not subject to or can overcome or ignore - any external supra-personal non-physical (non-temporal) force or forces, and thus of how these separated human beings have or can acquire the ability, the skill, to 'determine their own destiny/fate/life' by some means if the right method, or some methodology, or some tool - such as some idea or theory - can be found or developed, or if they develope their physical prowess/intelligence/cunning or acquire sufficient wealth/power/influence/followers.

Such a purely causal perception and causal understanding of living beings - lacking as it does an awareness of, an appreciation and a feeling for the numinous, or wilfully ignoring the numinous - is the genesis of ὕβρις and can thus bring-into-being the τύραννος [4].

An example of this reliance on causal perception and causal understanding is Oedipus, as described by Sophocles in Oedipus Tyrannus. In his singular desire to find the killer of Laius, Oedipus oversteps the due limits, and upsets the natural balance both within, and external to, himself. He is blinded by mere causality (a linear thinking) and subsumed by personal feelings – by his overwhelming desire for a simple cause-and-effect solution to the plague and his prideful belief that he, a mortal, a strong man, and master of the riddle of the Sphinx, can find or derive a solution. What results is tragedy, suffering, for himself and for others.

> ὦ πάτρας Θήβης ἔνοικοι, λεύσσετ᾽, Οἰδίπους ὅδε,
> ὃς τὰ κλείν᾽ αἰνίγματ᾽ ᾔδει καὶ κράτιστος ἦν ἀνήρ,
> οὗ τίς οὐ ζήλῳ πολιτῶν ἦν τύχαις ἐπιβλέπων,
> εἰς ὅσον κλύδωνα δεινῆς συμφορᾶς ἐλήλυθεν.
> ὥστε θνητὸν ὄντα κείνην τὴν τελευταίαν ἰδεῖν
> ἡμέραν ἐπισκοποῦντα μηδέν᾽ ὀλβίζειν, πρὶν ἂν
> τέρμα τοῦ βίου περάσῃ μηδὲν ἀλγεινὸν παθών.

> You natives of Thebes: Observe – here is Oedipus,
> He who understood that famous enigma and was a strong man:
> What clansman did not behold that fortune without envy?
> But what a tide of problems have come over him!
> Therefore, look toward that ending which is for us mortals,
> To observe that particular day – calling no one lucky until,
> Without the pain of injury, they are conveyed beyond life's ending.

> (Oedipus Tyrannus, vv. 1524-1530)

Another example is Creon, as described by Sophocles in his Antigone. Creon's pride and stubbornness, and his rigid adherence to his own, causal (temporal), mortal, edict – which overturns an ancestral custom established and maintained to 'please the gods' and implement a natural edict of the gods designed to give and maintain balance, harmony, among the community – leads to tragedy, to suffering.

The same thing occurred to Odysseus, who for all his prowess and mortal cunning could not contrive to return to his homeland as he wished nor save his friends, and

> κπολλὰ δ᾿ ὅ γ᾿ ἐν πόντῳ πάθεν ἄλγεα ὃν κατὰ θυμόν,
> ἀρνύμενος ἥν τε ψυχὴν καὶ νόστον ἑταίρων.
> ἀλλ᾿ οὐδ᾿ ὣς ἑτάρους ἐρρύσατο, ἱέμενός περ:
> αὐτῶν γὰρ σφετέρῃσιν ἀτασθαλίῃσιν ὄλοντο,
> νήπιοι, οἳ κατὰ βοῦς Ὑπερίονος Ἠελίοιο
> ἤσθιον: αὐτὰρ ὁ τοῖσιν ἀφείλετο νόστιμον ἦμαρ.

> ...whose vigour, at sea, was weakened by many afflictions
> As he strove to win life for himself and return his comrades to their homes.
> But not even he, for all this yearning, could save those comrades
> For they were destroyed by their own immature foolishness
> Having devoured the cattle of Helios, that son of Hyperion,
> Who plucked from them the day of their returning.

> (Homer, Odyssey, vv.3-9)

Such emphasis by mortals on causality, arising from a lack of the acausal, the numinous, perspective that empathy and πάθει μάθος provide, is in effect an ignoring of, a wilful defiance of, or a forgetfulness of, the natural balance, of our own nature, and of the gods. Expressed un-theistically, it is a lack of, or a covering-up of, or an ignorance of, the the nature of Being and of beings, of who and why we are, and why wu-wei is a wise way to live.

Our nature - which empathy and πάθει μάθος can reveal - is that of a mortal being veering between σωφρονεῖν (thoughtful reasoning, and thus fairness) and ὕβρις.

As Sophocles expressed it:

> πολλὰ τὰ δεινὰ κοὐδὲν ἀνθρώπου δεινότερον πέλει...
>
> σοφόν τι τὸ μηχανόεν τέχνας ὑπὲρ ἐλπίδ᾿ ἔχων
> τοτὲ μὲν κακόν, ἄλλοτ᾿ ἐπ᾿ ἐσθλὸν ἕρπει

> There exists much that is strange, yet nothing
> Has more strangeness than a human being...
> Beyond his own hopes, his cunning
> In inventive arts - he who arrives
> Now with dishonour, then with chivalry

> Antigone, v.334, vv.365-366

Yet as empathy and πάθει μάθος also reveal, our nature is such that we also have hope and a choice. We can choose to be fair, rational, beings who appreciate and cultivate σωφρονεῖν; who appreciate the numinous and ἁρμονίη and who understand ὕβρις for the error, the misfortune, the unbalance, it is. Or we can, like Oedipus, Creon, Aegisthus, and the comrades of Odysseus, foolishly, recklessly, veer toward and embrace ἔρις and ὕβρις.

We can appreciate the numinous - be wary of Μοῖραι τρίμορφοι μνήμονές τ᾽ Ἐρινύες. We can kindle and rekindle the 'fire of reason', and appreciate that when 'more is obtained than is necessary it is not kept'. Or we can take short-cuts, foolishly overladen ourselves, and in our recklessness believe we are immune to injury:

> τὸν δ᾽ ἄνευ λύρας ὅμως ὑμνῳδεῖ
> θρῆνον Ἐρινύος αὐτοδίδακτος ἔσωθεν
> θυμός, οὐ τὸ πᾶν ἔχων
> ἐλπίδος φίλον θράσος.
> σπλάγχνα δ᾽ οὔτοι ματᾴ-
> ζει πρὸς ἐνδίκοις φρεσὶν
> τελεσφόροις δίναις κυκώμενον κέαρ.
> εὔχομαι δ᾽ ἐξ ἐμᾶς
> ἐλπίδος ψύθη πεσεῖν
> ἐς τὸ μὴ τελεσφόρον.
>
> μάλα γέ τοι τὸ μεγάλας ὑγιείας
> ἀκόρεστον τέρμα: νόσος γάρ
> γείτων ὁμότοιχος ἐρείδει.
> καὶ πότμος εὐθυπορῶν
> ἀνδρὸς ἔπαισεν ἄφαντον ἕρμα.
> καὶ πρὸ μέν τι χρημάτων
> κτησίων ὄκνος βαλὼν
> σφενδόνας ἀπ᾽ εὐμέτρου,
> οὐκ ἔδυ πρόπας δόμος
> πημονᾶς γέμων ἄγαν,
> οὐδ᾽ ἐπόντισε σκάφος.
> πολλά τοι δόσις ἐκ Διὸς ἀμφιλα-
> φής τε καὶ ἐξ ἀλόκων ἐπετειᾶν
> νῆστιν ὤλεσεν νόσον.
>
> τὸ δ᾽ ἐπὶ γᾶν πεσὸν ἅπαξ θανάσιμον
> πρόπαρ ἀνδρὸς μέλαν αἷμα τίς ἂν
> πάλιν ἀγκαλέσαιτ᾽ ἐπαείδων;
> οὐδὲ τὸν ὀρθοδαῆ
> τῶν φθιμένων ἀνάγειν
> Ζεὺς ἀπέπαυσεν ἐπ᾽ εὐλαβείᾳ;
> εἰ δὲ μὴ τεταγμένα
> μοῖρα μοῖραν ἐκ θεῶν
> εἶργε μὴ πλέον φέρειν,

προφθάσασα καρδία
γλῶσσαν ἂν τάδ᾽ ἐξέχει.
νῦν δ᾽ ὑπὸ σκότῳ βρέμει
θυμαλγής τε καὶ οὐδὲν ἐπελπομέν-
α ποτὲ καίριον ἐκτολυπεύσειν
ζωπυρουμένας φρενός.

And so, although I have no lyre, I sing:
For there is a desire, within me - a self-taught hymn
For one of those Furies,
With nothing at all to bring me
That cherished confidence - hope.
And my stomach is by no means idle -
In fairness, it is from achieving a judgement
That the beat of my heart continues to change.
And so there is this supplication of mine:
For this defeat of my hope to be false
So that, that thing cannot be achieved.

In truth, that frequently unsatisfied goddess, Health,
Has a limit - for Sickness, her neighbour,
Leans against their shared fence;
And it is the fate of the mortal who takes the short-cut
To strike the unseen reef.
And yet if - of those possessions previously acquired
A fitting amount is, through caution, cast forth by a sling,
Then the whole construction will not go under -
Injuriously over-loaded as it was -
Nor will its hull be filled, by the sea.
Often, the gifts from Zeus are abundant
And there is, then, from the yearly ploughing,
A death for famine's sickness.

But if once upon the earth there falls from
A mortal that death-making black blood -
What incantation can return it to his arms?
Not even he who was correctly-taught
How to bring back those who had died
Was allowed by Zeus to be without injury.
Were it not that Fate was ordained
By the gods to make it fated
That when more is obtained it is not kept,
My heart would have been first
To let my tongue pour forth these things.

But now, in darkness, it murmurs,
Painfully-desiring, and having no hope of when
There will be an opportunity to bring this to an end,
Rekindling the fire of reason.

Aeschylus, Agamemnon, vv.990-1033

The Error of The-Separation-of-Otherness

The essence of the faculty of empathy is συμπάθεια with other living beings and which συμπάθεια involves a translocation of ourselves for a duration or durations of causal moments. There is thus a perception of the acausal, the numinous, reality underlying the causal division of beings, existents, into separate, causal-separated, objects and the subject-object relationship which is or has been assumed by means of the process of causal ideation to exist between such causally-separate beings. That is, and for instance, the implied or assumed causal separateness of living beings - the-separation-of-otherness - is causal appearance and not an expression of the true nature of Being and beings.

The-separation-of-otherness obscures and disrupts our relation to ψυχή and thus obscures the nature of our being and the nature of Being itself, and amounts to ὕβρις. For, in place of an understanding, a knowing, and thus an appreciation and acceptance of what is numinous - and thus of the natural balance and of what/whom we should respect - the-separation-of-otherness results in the positing of abstract categories/idealised forms to which we, as living beings, are assigned and which categories and forms are regarded as what we should aspire to and/or compare ourselves to and what we are judged by or judge ourselves by.

In classical terms, the natural balance and those whom we should respect - manifest in ψυχή and θεοί and Μοῖραι τρίμορφοι μνήμονές τ' Ἐρινύες and δαιμόνων and in those sacred places guarded or watched over by δαιμόνων - are arrogantly replaced by human manufactured, and fallible, ideations and which ideations do not in any way re-present the nature, the φύσις, of our being, the φύσις of other living beings, and φύσις of Being, and which φύσις is one of the living connexions, the numinosity, of ψυχή and thus of the Cosmic Perspective, a nature manifest, for we mortals, in an appreciation of the numinous and thus in living in a certain way because we understand the nature, the importance, of δίκη, of fairness, of not being excessive.

The result of such ὕβρις - of the-separation-of-otherness and of the arrogance assigning living beings to and judging them by lifeless abstractions, ideations; of neglecting θεοί and Μοῖραι τρίμορφοι μνήμονές τ' Ἐρινύες and δαιμόνων - is ἔρις: strife, discord, disruption, conflict, suffering, misfortune, and a loss of ψυχή and ἁρμονίη.

As Aeschylus mentioned, over two thousand years ago:

ἔστω δ᾽ ἀπή-
μαντον, ὥστ᾽ ἀπαρκεῖν
εὖ πραπίδων λαχόντα.
οὐ γὰρ ἔστιν ἔπαλξις
πλούτου πρὸς κόρον ἀνδρὶ
λακτίσαντι μέγαν Δίκας
βωμὸν εἰς ἀφάνειαν.

βιᾶται δ᾽ ἁ τάλαινα πειθώ,
προβούλου παῖς ἄφερτος ἄτας.
ἄκος δὲ πᾶν μάταιον. οὐκ ἐκρύφθη,
πρέπει δέ, φῶς αἰνολαμπές, σίνος...

λιτᾶν δ᾽ ἀκούει μὲν οὖτις θεῶν:
τὸν δ᾽ ἐπίστροφον τῶν
φῶτ᾽ ἄδικον καθαιρεῖ

For unharmed is the one
Who rightly reasons that what is sufficient
Is what is allotted to him.
For there is no protection
In riches for the man of excess
Who stamps down the great altar of the goddess, Judgement,
In order to hide it from view.

But vigorously endures Temptation -
That already-decided daughter of unbearable Misfortune.
And all remedies are in vain.
Not concealed, but conspicuous -
A harsh shining light -
Is the injury...

But not one of the gods hears the supplications:
Instead, they take down those persons
Who, lacking fairness, turn their attentions to such things.

Aeschylus, Agamemnon. vv.379-389, vv. 396-402

IV
An Appreciation of The Numinous

Empathy by its very nature - by its relocation, translocation, of ourselves into,
and συμπάθεια with, the living other - naturally inclines us toward compassion,

for to intentionally harm the living other is to feel, to know, that harm. Such harming might also upset, unbalance, hinder, or harm, the ψυχή we share with that and with other living beings and so in some way cause, or contribute to, or result in harm, suffering, or misfortune to us and/or to others now or on some future occasion or occasions.

In effect, compassion is a means to maintain ἁρμονίη and the natural balance of Life and thus to aid or contribute to our own ἁρμονίη and well-being as well as that of others.

Empathy - like πάθει μάθος - also inclines us toward treating other human beings as we ourselves would wish to be treated; that is it inclines us toward fairness, toward self-restraint, toward being well-mannered, and toward an appreciation and understanding of innocence, with innocence being regarded as an attribute of those who, being personally unknown to us, are therefore unjudged by us and who thus are given the benefit of the doubt. For this presumption of innocence of others – until direct personal experience, and individual and empathic knowing of them, prove otherwise – is the fair, the reasoned, the numinous thing to do.

Thus morality is, for The Way of Pathei-Mathos, a result of individuals using the faculty of empathy; a consequence of the insight and the understanding (the acausal knowing) that empathy provides for individuals in the immediacy-of-the-moment. Or, expressed another way, morality resides not in some abstract theory or some moralistic schemata presented in some written text which individuals have to accept and try and conform or aspire to, but rather in personal virtues that arise or which can arise naturally through empathy, πάθει μάθος, and thus from an awareness and appreciation of the numinous. Personal virtues such as compassion and fairness, and εὐταξία, that quality of self-restraint, of a balanced, well-mannered conduct especially under adversity or duress, of which Cicero wrote:

> Haec autem scientia continentur ea, quam Graeci εὐταξίαν nominant, non hanc, quam interpretamur modestiam, quo in verbo modus inest, sed illa est εὐταξία, in qua intellegitur ordinis conservatio
>
> Those two qualities are evident in that way described by the Greeks as εὐταξίαν although what is meant by εὐταξία is not what we mean by the moderation of the moderate, but rather what we consider is restrained behaviour...
>
> De Officiis, Liber Primus, 142

In practice, therefore, justice is not some abstract concept, some ideation, which it is believed can and should be administered by others and requiring the individual to accept, passively or willingly, some external authority. Rather, justice, like εὐταξία, like goodness, is numinous, living in the individual who - because of empathy, πάθει μάθος, awareness and appreciation of the numinous -

is inclined to be fair, who is capable of restraint especially under adversity or duress; the individual of σωφρονεῖν who thus "can tell inner character from outer" and who thus has those personal qualities which can be expressed by one word: honour.

The Numinous Balance of Honour

In many ways, the personal virtue of honour, and the cultivation of wu-wei, are - together - a practical, a living, manifestation of our understanding and appreciation of the numinous; of how to live, to behave, as empathy intimates we can or should in order to avoid committing the folly, the error, of ὕβρις, in order not to cause suffering, and in order to re-present, to acquire, ἁρμονίη.

For personal honour is essentially a presencing, a grounding, of ψυχή - of Life, of our φύσις - occurring when the insight (the knowing) of a developed empathy inclines us toward a compassion that is, of necessity, balanced by σωφρονεῖν and in accord with δίκη.

This balancing of compassion - of the need not to cause suffering - by σωφρονεῖν and δίκη is perhaps most obvious on that particular occasion when it may be judged necessary to cause suffering to another human being. That is, in honourable self-defence. For it is natural - part of our reasoned, fair, just, human nature - to defend ourselves when attacked and (in the immediacy of the personal moment) to valorously, with chivalry, act in defence of someone close-by who is unfairly attacked or dishonourably threatened or is being bullied by others, and to thus employ, if our personal judgement of the circumstances deem it necessary, lethal force.

This use of force is, importantly, crucially, restricted - by the individual nature of our judgement, and by the individual nature of our authority - to such personal situations of immediate self-defence and of valorous defence of others, and cannot be extended beyond that, for to so extend it, or attempt to extend it beyond the immediacy of the personal moment of an existing physical threat, is an arrogant presumption - an act of ὕβρις - which negates the fair, the human, presumption of innocence [15] of those we do not personally know, we have no empathic knowledge of, and who present no direct, immediate, personal, threat to us or to others nearby us.

Such personal self-defence and such valorous defence of another in a personal situation are in effect a means to restore the natural balance which the unfair, the dishonourable, behaviour of others upsets. That is, such defence fairly, justly, and naturally in the immediacy of the moment corrects their error of ὕβρις resulting from their bad (their rotten) φύσις; a rotten character evident in their lack of the virtue, the skill, of σωφρονεῖν. For had they possessed that virtue, and if their character was not bad, they would not have undertaken such a dishonourable attack.

Wu-Wei and The Cultivation of Humility

The knowledge, the understanding, the intuition, the insight that is wu-wei is a knowledge, an understanding, that can be acquired from empathy, πάθει μάθος, and by a knowing of and an appreciation of the numinous.

This knowledge and understanding, being of the wholeness, is that of the healthy, the interior, inward, and personal balance beyond the separation of beings – beyond πόλεμος and ὕβρις and thus beyond ἔρις; beyond the separation and thence the strife, the discord, which abstractions, ideations, encourage and indeed which they manufacture, bring-into-being. Among these ideations - and one which can often distance us from an appreciation of the numinous and thus from ἁρμονίη - is that of a measured Time of fixed durations; and one which thus has a tendency to both artificially apportion out our lives, urge us to hastily strive for some ideation, and cause us to live and/or work at an artificial, un-harmonious, pace.

Empathy, wu-wei, πάθει μάθος, and a knowing of and an appreciation of the numinous, also incline us toward the cultivation of humility as a prerequisite for us not to repeat our errors of ὕβρις, or the ὕβρις of others, and which mistakes of ὕβρις - ours and/or of others - we either are personally aware of or can become aware of through the recorded πάθει μάθος of our human cultures, manifest as this transmitted knowledge and personal learning often is in literature, Art, poetry, myths, legends, and music.

For our personal πάθει μάθος makes us aware of, makes us feel, know, remember, in a very personal sense, our fallibility, our mortality, our mistakes, our errors, our wrong deeds, the suffering we have caused, the harm we have done and inflicted; how much we personally have contributed to discord, strife, sorrow. Similarly, our appreciation of the numinous, together with empathy and the cultivation of wu-wei, makes us aware of, and feel, and understand, ὕβρις and the errors of ὕβρις in others past and present.

There is then, or there develops or there can develope, a personal inclination toward σωφρονεῖν; toward being fair, toward rational deliberation, toward a lack of haste, toward a living numinously. Toward a balanced judgement, and honour, and a knowing and appreciation of the wisdom that the only effective, long-lasting, change and reform that does not cause suffering - that is not redolent of ὕβρις - is the one that changes human beings in an individual way by personal example and/or because of πάθει μάθος, and thus interiorly changes what, in them, predisposes them, or inclines them toward, doing or what urges them to do, what is dishonourable, undignified, unfair, and uncompassionate.

That is what, individually, changes or rebalances bad φύσις and thus brings-into-being, or restores, good φύσις.

Conclusion - The Way of Pathei-Mathos

It is the cultivation by individuals of empathy, of wu-wei, of a reasoned judgement, combined with (i) an appreciation of the numinous and of our accumulated pathei-mathos - evident, for example, in Hellenic culture, in other cultures, and often manifest in Art, literature, music, myths, legends, poetry - and (ii) the living of a compassionate life balanced by honour, which are the whole of The Way of Pathei-Mathos.

The Way of Pathei-Mathos is thus an ethical, an interior, a personal, a non-political, a non-religious, a non-interfering, way of individual reflexion and individual change.

There is nothing else. No given, no required, praxis. No 'secret wisdom' or 'secret teachings', no enlightenment to be taught. No methodology, no theology, and no need for faith or belief. There are no theories, no goals, no dogma, no texts and no one to be revered.

Part Three

Some Personal Musings On Empathy
In relation to the philosophy of πάθει μάθος

Empathy and The Individual

The first axiom of the philosophy of pathei-mathos is:

> That human beings possess a mostly latent perceptive faculty, the
> faculty of empathy - ἐμπάθεια - which when used, or when developed
> and used, can provide us with a particular type of knowing, a
> particular type of knowledge, and especially a certain knowledge
> concerning the φύσις (the physis, the nature or character) of human
> beings and other living beings. [19]

Being a natural faculty - like sight and hearing - empathy is personal, individual,
and thus depends on and relates to what-is, and/or who-is, nearby: in range of
our empathy. Thus the knowing we acquire or can acquire by empathy is a
personal knowing just as seeing and listening to a person speaking is a personal
knowing acquired directly in the immediacy-of-the-moment. If, however, a
person be out of range of our empathy, and we have no previous empathic or
personal encounters with them, they are empathically and personally unknown
to us and therefore, since we have no knowledge or intimation of their physis,
their character, we cannot fairly assess them and should accord them 'the
benefit of the doubt' since this presumption of the innocence of others – until
direct personal experience, and individual and empathic knowing of them, prove
otherwise – is the fair, the reasoned, the moral, the empathic, thing to do.

For empathy, according to the philosophy of pathei-mathos, is considered the
primary means whereby we can fairly asses [20] - that is, fairly judge - a person
and thus know them (their physis) as they are, with this knowing, by the nature
of our as yet undeveloped and underused faculty of empathy, of necessity
requiring a personal and a direct experience of them extending over a period of
time. In effect, our initial intuitions are either confirmed or modified by such
direct contact, rather as most humans may require several periods of reading or
of the hearing of some lengthy text in order to commit it to memory and be able
to reproduce it, aurally or in writing.

There is thus what may be described as the empathic scale: that which or those who are reachable, knowable, by means of, in range of, our empathy; and it is this scale which, in essence, may be said to be a measure, a function and expression, of our humanity; which reveals, discovers, physis and thus what is important about ourselves, about other human beings, and about the other life with which we share this planet. Beyond the reach of empathy is the physis of beings we do not (as yet) personally know and we have to admit we do not know, and so cannot and should not be sure about or make claims about or formulate some theory or opinion about.

Everything others associate with an individual, or ascribe to an individual, or use to describe or to denote an individual, or even how an individual denotes or describes themselves, are not relevant, and have no bearing on our understanding, our knowledge, of that individual and thus - morally - should be ignored, for it is our personal knowing of them which is necessary, important, valid, fair. For assessment of another - by the nature of assessment and the nature of empathy - can only be personal, direct, individual. Anything else is biased prejudgement or prejudice or unproven assumption.

This means that we approach them - we view them - without any prejudice, without any expectations, and without having made any assumptions concerning them, and as a unique, still unknown, still undiscovered, individual person: as 'innocent' until proven, until revealed by their actions and behaviour to be, otherwise. Furthermore, empathy - the acausal perception/knowing and revealing of physis - knows nothing of temporal things and human manufactured abstractions/categories such as assumed or assigned ethnicity; nothing of gender; nothing of what is now often termed 'sexual preference/orientation'. Nothing of politics, or religion. Nothing of some disability someone may suffer from; nothing of social status or wealth; nothing regarding occupation (or lack of one). Nothing regarding the views, the opinions, of others concerning someone. For empathy is just empathy, a perception different from our other senses such as sight and hearing, and a perception which provides us, or which can provide us, with a unique perspective, a unique type of knowing, a unique (acausal) connexion to the external world and especially to other human beings.

Empathy - and the knowing that derives from it - thus transcends 'race', politics, religion, gender, sexual orientation, occupation, wealth (or lack of it), 'status', and all the other things and concepts often used to describe, to denote, to prejudge, to classify, a person; so that to judge someone - for example - by and because of their political views (real or assumed) or by their religion or by their sexual orientation is an act of hubris [ὕβρις].

In practice, therefore, in the revealing of the physis of a person, the political views, the religion, the gender, the perceived ethnicity, of someone are irrelevant. It is a personal knowing of them, the perception of their physis by empathy, and an acceptance of them as - and getting to know them as - a unique individual which are important and considered moral; for they are one emanation of the Life of which we ourselves are but one other finite and fallible part.

Concerning The Error of Extremism

Extremism - as defined and understood by the philosophy of pathei-mathos - is a modern example of the error of hubris. An outward expression - codified in an ideology - of a bad individual physis (of a bad or faulty or misguided or underdeveloped/unmatured individual nature); of a lack of inner balance in individuals; of a lack of empathy and of pathei-mathos.

There is thus, in extremists, an ignorance of the true nature of Being and beings, and a lack of appreciation of or a wilful rejection of the numinous, as well as a distinct lack of or an aversion to personal humility, for it is the nature of the extremist that they are convinced and believe that 'they know' that the ideology/party/movement/group/faith that they accept or adhere to - or the leader that they follow - have/has the right answers, the correct solutions, to certain problems which they faithfully assert exist in society and often in human beings.

This conviction, this arrogance of belief, or this reliance on the assessment of someone else (some leader), combined with a lack of empathy and a lack of the insight and the self-knowing wrought by pathei-mathos, causes or greatly enhances an existing inner/interior dissatisfaction (an unbalance, a lack of harmony) within them in regard to what-is, so that some vision, some ideal, of the future - of society - becomes more important to them, more real, more meaningful, than people, than life, as people and life are now. Thus, they with their ideology, their faith, with and because of their dissatisfaction, possess or develope an urge to harshly interfere, continually finding fault with people, with society, with life itself, and so strive - mostly violently, hatefully, unethically, and with prejudice and often with anger - to undermine, to violently change, to 'revolutionize', or to destroy, what-is.

In simple terms, extremists fail to understand, to appreciate, to know, to apprehend, what is important about human beings and human living; what the simple reality, the simple nature, the real physis, of the majority of human beings and of society is and are, and thus what innocence means and implies. That is, there is a failure to know, to appreciate, what is good, and natural and numinous and innocent, in respect of human beings and of society. A failure to know, a failure to appreciate, a failure to feel what it is that empathy and pathei-mathos provide: the wisdom of our personal nature and personal needs; of our physis as rational - as balanced - human beings possessed of certain qualities, certain virtues, or capable of developing balance, capable of developing certain qualities, certain virtues, and thus having or of developing the ability to live in a certain manner: with fairness, with love, and without hatred and prejudice.

What is good, and natural - what should thus be appreciated, and respected, and not profaned by the arrogance (the hubris) of the extremist, and what empathy and pathei-mathos reveal - are the desire for personal love and the need to be loyally loved; the need for a family and the bonds of love within a family that lead to the desire to protect, care for, work for, and if necessary defend one's loved ones. The desire for a certain security and stability and peace, manifest in a home, in sufficiency of food, in playfulness, in friends, in tolerance, in a lack of danger. The need for the dignity, the self-respect, that work, that giving love and being loved, provide.

Our societies have evolved, painfully slowly, to try and provide such simple, such human, such natural, such ineluctably personal, things; to allow opportunities for such things; and have so evolved often because of individuals naturally gifted with empathy or who were inspired by their own pathei-mathos or that of others, and often and thus also so evolved because of the culture that such societies encouraged and sometimes developed, being as such culture was - via, for example, literature, music, memoirs, poetry, Art - the recorded/aural pathei-mathos and empathic understanding of others often combined with the recorded/aural pathei-mathos and the empathic understanding of others in other societies. A pathei-mathos and an understanding that may form or in some manner express the ethos of a society, and thence become an inspiration for certain laws intended to express, in a society, what is considered to be moral and thus provide and maintain or at least aid valued human and personal qualities such as the desire for stability, peace, a loving home, sufficiency of food, and the need for the dignity of work.

But as I mentioned in some other musings regarding my own lamentable extremist past:

> " Instead of love we, our selfish, our obsessed, our extremist kind, engendered hate. Instead of peace, we engendered struggle, conflict, killing. Instead of tolerance we engendered intolerance. Instead fairness and equality we engendered dishonour and discrimination. Instead of security we produced, we encouraged, revolution, violence, change.
>
> The problem, the problems, lay inside us, in our kind, not in 'the world', not in others. We, our kind - we the pursuers of, the inventors of, abstractions, of ideals, of ideologies; we the selfish, the arrogant, the hubriatic, the fanatics, the obsessed - were and are the main causes of hate, of conflict, of suffering, of inhumanity, of violence.

Century after century, millennia after millennia."

For perhaps one of the worst consequences of the extremism of extremists - of modern hubris in general - is, or seems to me to be, the loss of what is personal, and thus what is human; the loss of the empathic, the human, scale of things; with what is personal, human, empathic, being or becoming displaced, scorned, forgotten, obscured, or a target for destruction and (often violent) replacement by something supra-personal such as some abstract political/religious notion or concept, or some ideal, or by some prejudice and some often violent intolerance regarding human beings we do not personally know because beyond the range of our empathy.

That is, the human, the personal, the empathic, the natural, the immediate, scale of things - a tolerant and a fair acceptance of what-is - is lost and replaced by an artificial scale posited by some ideology or manufactured by some τύραννος (tyrannos); a scale in which the suffering of individuals, and strife, are regarded as inevitable, even necessary, in order for 'victory to be achieved' or for some ideal or plan or agenda or manifesto to be implemented. Thus the good, the stability, that exists within society is ignored, with the problems of society - real, imagined, or manufactured by propaganda - trumpeted. There is then incitement to disaffection, with harshness and violent change of and within society regarded as desirable or necessary in order to achieve preset, predetermined, and always 'urgent' goals and aims, since slow personal reform and change in society - that which appreciates and accepts the good in an existing society and in people over and above the problems and the bad - is anathema to extremists, anathema to their harsh intolerant empathy-lacking nature and to their hubriatic striving:

> " [The truth] in respect of the societies of the West, and especially of societies such as those currently existing in America and Britain - is that for all their problems and all their flaws they seem to be much better than those elsewhere, and certainly better than what existed in the past. That is, that there is, within them, a certain tolerance; a certain respect for the individual; a certain duty of care; and certainly still a freedom of life, of expression, as well as a standard of living which, for perhaps the majority, is better than elsewhere in the world and most certainly better than existed there and elsewhere in the past.
>
> In addition, there are within their structures - such as their police forces, their governments, their social and governmental institutions - people of good will, of humanity, of fairness, who strive to do what is good, right. Indeed, far more good people in such places than bad people, so that a certain balance, the balance of goodness, is

maintained even though occasionally (but not for long) that balance may seem to waver somewhat.

Furthermore, many or most of the flaws, the problems, within such societies are recognized and openly discussed, with a multitude of people of good will, of humanity, of fairness, dedicating themselves to helping those affected by such flaws, such problems. In addition, there are many others trying to improve those societies, and to trying find or implement solutions to such problems, in tolerant ways which do not cause conflict or involve the harshness, the violence, the hatred, of extremism." Notes on The Politics and Ideology of Hate (Part Two)

Yet it is just such societies - societies painfully and slowly crafted by the sacrifice and the goodness of multitudes of people of good will, of humanity, of fairness - that extremists with their harsh intolerant empathy-lacking nature, their hubriatic striving, their arrogant certainty of belief, their anger and their need to harshly interfere, seek to undermine, overthrow, and destroy.

No Hubriatic Striving, No Impersonal Interference

Since the range of empathy is limited to the immediacy-of-the-moment and to personal interactions, and, together with pathei-mathos, is a primary means to reveal the nature of Being and beings - and since the learning wrought by pathei-mathos and pathei-mathos itself is and are direct and personal - then part of the knowledge, the understanding, that empathy and pathei-mathos reveal and provide is the wisdom of physis and of humility. That is, of the empathic scale of things and of acceptance of our limitations of personal knowing and personal understanding. Of (i) the unwisdom, the hubris, of arrogantly making assumptions about who and what are beyond the range of our empathy and outside of our personal experience, and (ii) of the unwisdom, the hubris, of adhering to some ideology or some belief or to some tyrannos and allowing that ideology or that belief or that tyrannos to usurp the personal judgement, the personal assessment, that empathy and pathei-mathos reveal and provide.

This acceptance of the empathic - of the human, the personal - scale of things and of our limitations as human beings is part of wu-wei. Of not-striving, and of not-interfering, beyond the purveu of our empathy and our pathei-mathos. Of personally and for ourselves discovering the nature, the physis, of beings; of personally working with and not against that physis, and of personally accepting that certain matters or many matters, because of our lack of personal knowledge and lack of personal experience of them, are unknown to us and therefore it is unwise, unbalanced, for us to have and express views or opinions concerning them, and hubris for us to adhere to and strive to implement some ideology which harshly deals with and manifests harsh views and harsh opinions concerning such personally unknown matters.

Thus what and who are beyond the purveu of empathy and beyond pathei-mathos is or should be of no urgent concern, of no passionate relevance, to the individual seeking balance, harmony, and wisdom, and in truth can be detrimental to finding wisdom and living in accord with the knowledge and understanding so discovered.

For wisdom, it seems to me, is simply a personal appreciation of the numinous, of innocence, of balance, of εὐταξία [21], of enantiodromia, and the personal knowing, the understanding, that empathy and pathei-mathos provide. An appreciation, a knowing, that is the genesis of a balanced personal judgement - of discernment – and evident in our perception of Being and beings: of how all living beings are emanations of ψυχή and of how the way of non-suffering causing moral change and reform both personal and social is the way of wu-wei. The way of personal, interior, change; of aiding, helping, assisting other individuals in a direct, a personal manner, and in practical ways, because our seeing is that of the human, the empathic, the muliebral, scale of things and not the scale of hubris, which is the scale either (i) of the isolated, egoist, striveful, unharmonious human being in thrall to their selfish masculous desires or (ii) of the human being unbalanced because in thrall to some tyrannos or to some harsh, extremist, ideology, and which harsh ideologies always manifest an unbalanced masculous, unempathic, nature redolent of that hubriatic certainty-of-knowing and that intolerant desire to interfere which mark and which have marked, and are and were the genesis of, the tyrannos.

Part Four

Enantiodromia and The Reformation of The Individual

The Muliebral and the Masculous

The third axiom of The Way of Pathei-Mathos is:

> That because of or following πάθει μάθος there is or there can be a
> change in, a development of, the nature, the character - the φύσις - of
> the person because of that revealing and that appreciation (or
> re-appreciation) of the numinous whose genesis is this πάθει μάθος,
> and which appreciation of the numinous includes an awareness of why
> ὕβρις is an error (often the error) of unbalance, of disrespect or
> ignorance (of the numinous), of a going beyond the due limits, and
> which ὕβρις itself is the genesis both of the τύραννος and of the
> modern error of extremism. For the tyrannos and the modern
> extremist (and their extremisms) embody and give rise to and
> perpetuate ἔρις and thus are a cause of, or contribute to and aid,
> suffering.

This change, this development of the individual, is or can be the result of a
process termed enantiodromia, which is the process of perceiving, feeling,
knowing, beyond causal appearance and the separation-of-otherness and thus
when what has become separated - or has been incorrectly perceived as
separated - returns to the wholeness, the unity, from whence it came forth.
When beings are understood in their correct relation to Being, beyond the
causal abstraction of different/conflicting ideated opposites, a relation manifest
in the cosmic perspective and thus a knowing of ourselves as but one fallible,
microcosmic, fragile, mortal, biological nexion connected to and not separate
from all other Life.

An important and a necessary part of enantiodromia involves a discovery, a knowing, an acceptance, and - as prelude - an interior balancing within themselves, of what has hitherto been perceived and designated as the apparent opposites described by terms such as 'muliebral' and 'masculous'. A perception of opposites manifested in ideations such as those concerning assumed traits of character, and assumed or 'ideal' rôles, behaviour, and occupations, assigned to each person, and especially historically in the prejudice of how the rôle - the duty - of men is or should be to lead, to control, to govern, to possess authority, to dominate, to be master.

The discovery of enantiodromia is of how such a designated and perceived dichotomy is but illusive, unnecessary, unhealthy, appearance, and does not therefore express either the natural, the real, nature (φύσις) of our personal character, our being, or the real nature, the Φύσις, of Being itself. In essence, this is the discovery, mentioned by Heraclitus [22], concerning Πόλεμος and γινόμενα πάντα κατ᾽ ἔριν καὶ χρεώμενα; that all beings are naturally born - become perceived as separate beings - because of ἔρις, and their genesis (their 'father') is Πόλεμος.

Thus the strife, the discord, often engendered by an external and by the internal (within the individual) clash between such apparent opposites as the 'muliebral' and 'masculous' is one that has naturally arisen due to misperception, due to the separation-of-otherness, as a result of a purely causal, egoist, apprehension of ourselves and of others; an error of perception that, as previously mentioned, empathy and πάθει μάθος can correct, and which correction reveals the truth of ψυχή and a knowing of the cosmic perspective.

One practical consequence of this misapprehension, this error of ὕβρις, concerning 'muliebral' and 'masculous' has been the distaste - even the hatred - of certain ideologies and religions and individuals for those whose personal love is for someone of the same gender. Another practical consequence is and has been the error of extremism, where what is masculous is emphasized to the detriment (internal, and external) of what is muliebral, and where, for example, as in many harsh ideologies, men and women are expected, encouraged - often forced, as for example in fascism - to assume some rôle based on or deriving from some manufactured abstraction, some ideation, concerning what is assumed to be or has been posited as 'the ideal man' or the 'ideal woman' in some idealized society or in some idealized 'nation'.

Furthermore, given that these attributes of personal character that have been termed 'muliebral' and 'masculous' are founded on an illusive apprehension of beings and Being - and on ideations (such as rôles, occupations, and so on) posited as a result of this misapprehension - they not symbolic, or mythological, or unconscious, or even archetypal in the sense of anima and animus.

A Natural Reformation

The balance attained by - which is - enantiodromia is that of simply feeling, accepting, discovering, the empathic, the human, the personal, scale of things and thus understanding our own fallibility-of-knowing, our limitations as a human being; that, in essence, αἰὼν παῖς ἐστι παίζων πεσσεύων· παιδὸς ἡ βασιληίη [23], that τὰ δὲ πάντα οἰακίζει Κεραυνός [24] and that Φύσις κρύπτεσθαι φιλεῖ [25].

Which in practical terms simply amounts to understanding, knowing, Being and the genesis, the φύσις, of beings. Or, expressed in terms of the philosophy of pathei-mathos, it amounts to wu-wei, and to the understanding that 'what and who' are out of range of our empathy and what and who we have no personal knowledge of, is and are of no concern, of no passionate relevance, for us, because 'beyond the control, the influence' of our own fallible, error-prone, nature, and should thus be regarded 'without prejudice', as 'innocent', and the subject of no opinion, no ideations, by us. That is, we accept empathy and pathei-mathos as our guide, and (i) we do not speculate about, do not manufacture our own ideations about, those whom and that which are beyond the purveu of our empathy; and (ii) we do not accept the ideations/abstractions of others concerning those whom and that which are beyond the purveu of our empathy, and who and which we have no direct personal experience of.

Thus the process, the discovery, the reformation, is a natural one that does not involve any theory, or dogma, or praxis, or require any faith or belief of any kind. There is the personal cultivation of empathy and wu-wei, and that is all. How then - for those not having endured a personal πάθει μάθος - might empathy and wu-wei be cultivated, and thus how might the natural balance be found/restored, thus allowing ψυχή to flourish, bringing ἁρμονίη and σωφρονεῖν?

We might let go of ideations, of causal abstractions, many or most of which only serve to try and distinguish us from them, from other living-beings, human or otherwise, and thus increase our illusion of separation. We might consider, ponder on, the cosmic perspective and learn to value tolerance and humility. We might muse on innocence and the nature of the good, for the good is simply what is fair; what is compassionate, what inclines us to appreciate the numinous and understand why ὕβρις is an error of unbalance. We might consider why, for example, the bad is just bad φύσις. Or a natural consequence of undeveloped, unformed, not-mature, unreformed φύσις. Of a lack of empathy, of a lack of εὐταξία, of little or no appreciation of, of no personal experience of, the numinous, leading thus to individuals doing what is unfair; what is harsh and unfeeling; what intentionally causes or contributes to suffering.

We could, for example, and perhaps importantly, learn from the culture of our society and that of others, for correctly appreciated such culture - as manifest, for example, in literature, music, memoirs, poetry, history, Art, and sometimes in myths and legends and religious allegories - is but the recorded/aural pathei-mathos and empathic understanding of others over decades, centuries, millennia.

Part Five

Society, Politics, Social Reform, and Pathei-Mathos

Modern Society and The Individual

Society, in the context of this essay, refers to 'modern societies' (especially those of the modern 'democratic' West) and means a collection of individuals who dwell, who live, in a particular area and who are subject to the same laws and the same institutions of authority. Modern society is thus a manifestation of The State, and which State is predicated on individuals actively or passively accepting some supra-personal authority [26].

In modern societies, change and reform are often therefore introduced or attempted by The State most usually: (1) on the basis of the manufacture of some law or laws which the individuals, and the established institutions, of the area governed by The State are expected to obey on pain of some type of individual punishment, financial and/or physically punitive (as in prison); or (2) by means of State-sponsored or State-introduced schemes such as, for example, the British National Health Service and which schemes are invariably enshrined in law.

The essence of such change and reform of a society - large-scale, effective, rapid change and reform in society - is therefore, for the majority of people, external, and most often derives from some posited or assumed or promised agenda of the government of the day; that is, derived from some political or social or economic theory, axiom, idea, or principle, posited by others, be these others, for example, politicians, or social/political/economic theorists/reformers (and so on).

There is thus a hierarchy of judgement involved, whatever political 'flavour' the government is assigned to, is assumed to represent, or claims it represents; with this hierarchy of necessity requiring the individual in society to either (i) relinquish their own judgement, being accepting of or acquiescing in (from whatever reason or motive such as desire to avoid punishment) the judgement of these others, or (ii) to oppose this 'judgement of others' either actively through some group, association, or movement (political, social, religious) or individually, with their being the possibility that some so opposing this 'judgement of others' may resort to using violent means against the established order.

Objectively, this process of change and reform by means of a hierarchy of judgement manifest in laws, and of State authority and power sufficient to enforce such laws, has resulted in fairly stable societies which are, for perhaps the majority of people, relatively peaceful, not overtly repressive, and - judged by the criteria of past societies and many non-Western societies - relatively prosperous.

Thus, while many problems - social and economic - remain and exist in such societies, with some such problems getting worse, such societies work reasonably well, contain an abundance of well-intentioned, moral, individuals, and appear to be better than the alternatives both tried in the past and theorized about. Hence it is not surprising that perhaps the majority of people within such societies favour solving such problems as do exist by existing social, political, and economic means; that is, by internal social, political, and economic, reform rather than by violent means and the advocacy of extremist ideologies.

Furthermore, many or most of the flaws, and the problems, within society are recognized and openly discussed, with a multitude of people of good will, of humanity, of fairness, committed to or interested in helping those affected by such flaws and problems, and thus not only trying to improve society but also to finding and implementing solutions in tolerant ways which do not cause conflict or involve the harshness, the violence, the hatred, the intolerance, of extremism.

For, while most large-scale, effective, rapid change and reform in society tends to be by enforceable State laws and State-sponsored schemes, change and reform also and significantly occurs and has occurred within society, albeit often more slowly, through the efforts of individuals and groups and organizations devoted to charitable, religious, or social causes and which individuals and groups and organizations by their very nature are invariably non-violent and often non-political. Furthermore, such non-violent, non-political, individuals and groups and organizations often become the inspiration for reform and change introduced by The State.

Some Problems of Modern Society

Before outlining a possible numinous approach to reform and change, based on the philosophy of pathei-mathos, it would perhaps be useful to outline some of the social problems that still beset modern societies. What therefore constitutes a social problem within a society? How is such a problem defined?

In essence, it is an undesirable circumstance or way of living that affects a number of people and which undesirable circumstance or way of living others in society are or become aware of; with what is undesirable being - according to the ethics of the philosophy of pathei-mathos [27] - that which is, or those who are, unfair; that which deprives or those whom deprive a human being of dignity and honour; and that which is and those who are uncompassionate.

Thus, among the many problems of modern societies are misogyny; ethnic and religious discrimination, hatred, and prejudice; and social/economic inequality.

For example, misogyny - from the Greek μισογύνης - is unfairness toward, and/or prejudice and discrimination against, women. Often, as in the past, this is a consequence of an existing prejudice in a man: for example, that men are somehow better than women, or that women are 'useful' only for or suited to certain things; or that the subservience of women, and thus their domination/control by men, is 'a natural and necessary' state of human existence.

Misogyny in individual practice often results in men being violent/domineering toward, or selfishly manipulative and controlling of, women; and thus in them treating women in a dishonourable, undignified, unfair, and uncompassionate way.

Similarly, a hatred or dislike of or discrimination against an individual or a group of individuals on the basis of their perceived or assumed ethnicity is treating that individual or group in a dishonourable, undignified, unfair, and uncompassionate way.

Thus such social problems are often the result, the consequence of, a lack of empathy in a person, with this lack of συμπάθεια with other human beings having often in the past been evident in the treatment of people and individuals by governments, States, and institutions, and often revealed in and through discriminatory, unfair, uncompassionate laws.

A Numinous and Non-Political Approach

Given that the concern of the philosophy of pathei-mathos is the individual and their interior, their spiritual, life, and given that (due to the nature of empathy and pathei-mathos) there is respect for individual judgement, the philosophy of pathei-mathos is apolitical, and thus not concerned with such matters as the theory and practice of governance, nor with changing or reforming society by political means.

For, as mentioned in *Part Two: Some Personal Musings On Empathy,*

> " [the] acceptance of the empathic - of the human, the personal - scale of things and of our limitations as human beings is part of wu-wei. Of not-striving, and of not-interfering, beyond the purveu of our empathy and our pathei-mathos. Of personally and for ourselves discovering the nature, the physis, of beings; of personally working with and not against that physis, and of personally accepting that certain matters or many matters, because of our lack of personal knowledge and lack of personal experience of them, are unknown to us and therefore it is unwise, unbalanced, for us to have and express views or opinions concerning them, and hubris for us to adhere to and strive to implement some ideology which harshly deals with and manifests harsh views and harsh opinions concerning such personally unknown matters.
>
> Thus what and who are beyond the purveu of empathy and beyond pathei-mathos is or should be of no urgent concern, of no passionate relevance, to the individual seeking balance, harmony, and wisdom, and in truth can be detrimental to finding wisdom and living in accord with the knowledge and understanding so discovered. "

This means that there is no desire and no need to use any confrontational means to directly challenge and confront the authority of existing States since numinous reform and change is personal, individual, non-political, and not organized beyond a limited local level of people personally known. That is, it is of and involves individuals who are personally known to each other working together based on the understanding that it is inner, personal, change - in individuals, of their nature, their character - that is is the ethical, the numinous, way to solve such personal and social problems as exist and arise. That such inner change of necessity comes before any striving for outer change by whatever means, whether such means be termed or classified as political, social, economic, religious. That the only effective, long-lasting, change and reform is understood as the one that evolves human beings and thus changes what, in them, predisposes them, or inclines them toward, doing or what urges them to do, what is dishonourable, undignified, unfair, and uncompassionate.

In practice, this evolution means, in the individual, the cultivation and use of the faculty of empathy, and acquiring the personal virtues of compassion, honour, and love. Which means the inner reformation of individuals, as individuals.

Hence the basis for numinous social change and reform is aiding, helping, assisting individuals in a direct and personal manner, and in practical ways, with such help, assistance, and aid arising because we personally know or are personally concerned about or involved with those individuals or the situations those individuals find themselves in. In brief, being compassionate, empathic, understanding, sensitive, kind, and showing by personal example.

An Experience of The Numinous

The change that the philosophy - the way - of pathei-mathos seeks to foster, to encourage, is the natural, slow, interior and personal change within individuals; that is, the change of personal character by the individual developing and using their faculty of empathy and inclining toward being compassionate and honourable by nature. In essence, this is a numinous - a spiritual - change in people, a change of perspective, quite different from the supra-personal social change based on laws desired by modern States and by those who champion or who employ political, economic, and social theories regarding society, government, and the individual.

This interior personal change, by its numinous and ethical nature, is one that does not seek to reform society through politics or by any type of agitation, or through the use of force, or by means of any type of organization, social, political, economic, religious. Instead, such numinous change is the reform of individuals on a personal, individual, and cultural basis; by personal example and by individuals cultivating, in accordance with wu-wei, conditions and circumstances whereby they themselves and others can move toward συμπάθεια with other human beings through a personal knowing and experience of the numinous. Such a knowing and experience of the numinous can be cultivated by a variety of means, for example by harmonious surroundings; through an appreciation of, and a living in balance with, Nature; by love and respect and manners and a desire for peace; by periods of interior and exterior silence; through culture and thus through music, Art, literature, an understanding of history, and through respect for and tolerance of the many religions and spiritual Ways which have arisen over millennia and which may manifest the numinous or something of the numinous.

Part Six

The Change of Enantiodromia

The Meaning of Enantiodromia

The unusual compound Greek word ἐναντιοδρομίας occurs in a summary of the philosophy of Heraclitus by Diogenes Laërtius:

> πάντα δὲ γίνεσθαι καθ᾽ εἱμαρμένην καὶ διὰ τῆς ἐναντιοδρομίας ἡρμόσθαι τὰ ὄντα (ix. 7)

This unusual word is usually translated as something like 'conflict of opposites' or 'opposing forces' which I consider are incorrect for several reasons.

Firstly, in my view, a transliteration should be used instead of some translation, for the Greek expression suggests something unique, something which exists in its own right as a principle or 'thing' and which uniqueness of meaning has a context, with both context and uniqueness lost if a bland translation is attempted. Lost, as the uniqueness, and context, of for example, δαιμόνων becomes lost if simply translated as 'spirits' (or worse, as 'gods'), or as the meaning of κακός in Hellenic culture is lost if mistranslated as 'evil'.

Second, the context seems to me to hint at something far more important than 'conflict of opposites', the context being the interesting description of the philosophy of Heraclitus before and after the word occurs, as given by Diogenes Laërtius:

> 1) ἐκ πυρὸς τὰ πάντα συνεστάναι

> 2) εἰς τοῦτο ἀναλύεσθαι

3) πάντα δὲ γίνεσθαι καθ᾽ εἰμαρμένην καὶ διὰ τῆς ἐναντιοδρομίας ἡρμόσθαι τὰ ὄντα

4) καὶ πάντα ψυχῶν εἶναι καὶ δαιμόνων πλήρη

The foundation/base/essence of all beings ['things'] is pyros to which they return, with all [of them] by genesis appropriately apportioned [separated into portions] to be bound together again by enantiodromia, and all filled/suffused/vivified with/by ψυχή and Dæmons.

This raises several interesting questions, not least concerning ψυχή and δαιμόνων, but also regarding the sense of πυρὸς. Is pyros here a philosophical principle - such as ψυχή - or used as in fragment 43, the source of which is also Diogenes Laërtius:

ὕβριν χρὴ σβεννύναι μᾶλλον ἢ πυρκαϊὴν (ix 2)

Better to deal with your hubris before you confront that fire

Personally, I incline toward the former, of some principle being meant, given the context, and the generalization - ἐκ πυρὸς τὰ πάντα. In respect of ψυχῶν καὶ δαιμόνων I would suggest that what is implied is the numinous, our apprehension of The Numen, and which numen is the source of ψυχή and the origin of Dæmons. For a δαίμων is not one of the pantheon of major Greek gods – θεοί - but another type of divinity (that is, another emanation of the numen; another manifestation of the numinous) who might be assigned by those numinous gods to bring good fortune or misfortune to human beings and/or who watch over certain human beings and especially over particular numinous (sacred) places.

Thus the above summary of the philosophy of Heraclitus might be paraphrased as:

The foundation of all beings is Pyros to which they return, with all by genesis appropriately apportioned to be bound together again by enantiodromia, with all beings suffused with [are emanations of] the numen.

Furthermore, hubris disrupts - and conceals - our appreciation of the numen, our appreciation of ψυχή and of Dæmons: of what is numinous and what/whom we should respect. A disruption that makes us unbalanced, makes us disrespect the numinous and that of the numinous (such as δαιμόνων and θεοί and sacred places), and which unbalance enantiodromia can correct, with enantiodromia suggesting a confrontation - that expected dealing with our hubris necessary in order to return to Pyros, the source of beings. Here, Pyros is understood not as we understand 'fire' - and not even as some sort of basic physical element among other elements such as water - but rather as akin to both the constant 'warmth and the light of the Sun' (that brings life) and the sudden lightning that, as from Zeus, can serve as warning (omen) and retribution, and which can destroy and be a cause of devastating fire and thus also of the regeneration/rebuilding that often follows from such fires and from the learning, the respect, that arises from appreciating warnings (omens) from the gods. All of which perhaps explains fragment 64:

τὰ δὲ πάντα οἰακίζει Κεραυνός

All beings are guided by Lightning

Enantiodromia in the Philosophy of Pathei-Mathos

In the philosophy of pathei-mathos, enantiodromia is understood as the process - the natural change - that occurs or which can occur in a human being because of or following πάθει μάθος. For part of πάθει μάθος is a 'confrontational contest' - an interior battle - and an acceptance of the need to take part in this battle and 'face the consequences', one of which is learning the (often uncomfortable) truth about one's own unbalanced, strife-causing, nature.

If successful in this confrontation, there is or there can be a positive, moral, development of the nature, the character - the φύσις (physis) - of the person because of that revealing and that appreciation (or re-appreciation) of the numinous whose genesis is this pathei-mathos, and which appreciation includes an awareness of why ὕβρις is an error (often the error) of unbalance, of disrespect, of a going beyond the due limits, and which ὕβρις is the genesis of the τύραννος and of the modern error of extremism. For the tyrannos and the extremist (and their extremisms) embody and give rise to and perpetuate ἔρις [28].

Thus enantiodromia reveals the nature of, and restores in individuals, the natural balance necessary for ψυχή to flourish - which natural balance is δίκη as Δίκα [29] and which restoration of balance within the individual results in ἁρμονίη [30], manifest as ἁρμονίη is in the cultivation, in the individual, of wu-wei and σωφρονεῖν (a fair and balanced personal, individual, judgement).

Part Seven

The Abstraction of Change as Opposites and Dialectic

I - Opposites and Dialectic as Abstractions

For well over a hundred years there has been a belief that some kind of process, or dialectic, between or involving certain, particular, opposites might lead us to answer questions such as Quid est Veritas?, could lead to a certain understanding of ourselves, and may well express something of the true nature of reality, of Being itself. In varying degrees this belief is evident, for instance, in Hegel, Nietzsche (with his Wille zur macht), Marx, and those espousing the doctrine that has been termed Social Darwinism.

In addition, and for a much greater span of causal Time, this belief has been an essential part of certain religions where the process is often expressed eschatologically and in a conjectured conflict between the abstract opposites of 'good' and 'evil', God and Devil, and such things as demons and angels.

This notion of opposites, of two distinct, separate, things is much in evidence in Plato, and indeed, philosophically, the separation of beings from Being by the process of ideation and opposites may be said to have begun with Plato. For instance, he contrasts πόλεμος with στάσις (Conflict/strife contrasted with stasis/stability) thus:

> ἐπὶ μὲν οὖν τῇ τοῦ οἰκείου ἔχθρᾳ στάσις κέκληται, ἐπὶ δὲ τῇ τοῦ ἀλλοτρίου πόλεμος. Rep. V 470b

In respect of these two forms, Plato tries to explain that while there are two terms, two distinct namings - πόλεμος and στάσις - what are so denoted are not just two different names but express what he regards as the reality - the being, οὐσία - of two differing contrasted beings; that is, he posits what we would call two different ideations, or abstractions, creating an abstract (idealized) form for one and an abstract (idealized) form for the other.

Some centuries later, Diogenes Laërtius - apparently paraphrasing Heraclitus - wrote in his Lives of Eminent Philosophers:

πάντα δὲ γίνεσθαι καθ᾽ εἱμαρμένην καὶ διὰ τῆς ἐναντιοδρομίας ἡρμόσθαι τὰ ὄντα (ix. 7)

All by genesis is appropriately apportioned [separated into portions] with beings bound together again by enantiodromia [31].

Which might seem to suggest that a certain mis-understanding of Heraclitus [32]. the ideation of Plato and of later philosophers and theologians, was the genesis of abstractions and of this belief that a so-called conflict of opposites can lead to 'truth', and explain the nature of Being and beings.

However, this ideation, this development of abstractions, and this process of a dialectic, led to the philosophical error of the separation of beings from Being so that instead of the revealing that would answer Quid est Veritas? there is ὕβρις with the numinous authority of an individual πάθει μάθος replaced by adherence to some dogmatic dialectical process involving some assumed struggle/conflict. That is, by considering ἀρχὴ as the cause of the abstractions which are opposites and the origin of a dialectic, and which opposites, and which dialectic involving them, are said to manifest the nature of both our being and of Being itself.

This is an error because Πόλεμος is neither kampf nor conflict, but rather - as the quote from Diogenes Laërtius suggests - what lies behind or beyond Phainómenon; that is, non-temporal, non-causal, Being which, though we have have a natural tendency to separate into portions (that is, to perceive beings as only beings), beings themselves become revealed as bound together again by us facing up to the expected contest: that is, to our human nature and to knowing, to developing, to using, our faculty of reasoned judgement - σωφρονεῖν - to uncover, to reveal, via λόγος, the true nature of Δίκα and thus restore ἁρμονίη [33].

That is, instead of this abstraction of a dialectic there is, as I have suggested elsewhere:

A natural process of Change, of ἀρχὴ which we apprehend as Φύσις - as Heraclitus expressed in fragment 112:

σωφρονεῖν ἀρετὴ μεγίστη, καὶ σοφίη ἀληθέα λέγειν καὶ

ποιεῖν κατὰ φύσιν ἐπαίοντας.

This suggests that what is most excellent [ἀρετὴ] is thoughtful reasoning [σωφρονεῖν] – and that such thoughtful reasoning is a process which not only expresses and uncovers meaning, but which is also in accord with, in harmony or in sympathy with, φύσις – that is, with our own nature as mortals and with the nature of Being itself. [34]

II - The Error of Polemos as Kampf

In a fragment attributed to Heraclitus [35] Πόλεμος is generally regarded as a synonym for either kampf, or more generally, for war; with the fragment then considered to mean something such as: strife (or war) is the father of everything. This interpretation is said to compliment another fragment attributed to Heraclitus:

εἰδέναι δὲ χρὴ τὸν πόλεμον ἐόντα ξυνόν, καὶ δίκην ἔριν, καὶ γινόμενα πάντα κατ᾽ ἔριν καὶ χρεώμενα [χρεών]. Fragmentum 80.

This is generally considered to mean something abstract such as: war is everywhere and strife is justice and all that is arises and passes away because of strife.

However, I contend that this older understanding of - the accepted rendition of - Πόλεμος is a misinterpretation of Πόλεμος [36], and that rather than kampf (struggle), or a general type of strife, or what we now associate with the term war, Πόλεμος implies the acausality (a simultaneity) beyond our causal ideation, and which ideation has separated object from subject, and often abstracted them into seemingly conflicting opposites. Hence my interpretation of Fragmentum 53:

Πόλεμος πάντων μὲν πατήρ ἐστι, πάντων δὲ βασιλεύς, καὶ τοὺς μὲν θεοὺς ἔδειξε τοὺς δὲ ἀνθρώπους, τοὺς μὲν δούλους ἐποίησε τοὺς δὲ ἐλευθέρους.

Polemos our genesis, governing us all to bring forth some gods, some mortal beings with some unfettered yet others kept bound.

Hence also my interpretation of εἰδέναι δὲ χρὴ τὸν πόλεμον ἐόντα ξυνόν, καὶ δίκην ἔριν, καὶ γινόμενα πάντα κατ᾽ ἔριν καὶ χρεώμενα [χρεών] as:

One should be aware that Polemos pervades, with discord δίκη, and that beings are naturally born by discord. [37]

Thus the suggestion is that Πόλεμος is not some abstract 'war' or strife or kampf, but not only that which is or becomes the genesis of beings from Being, but also that which manifests as δίκη and accompanies ἔρις because it is the nature of Πόλεμος that beings, born because of and by ἔρις, can be returned to Being (become bound together - be whole - again).

For it is perhaps interesting that in the recounted tales of Greek mythology attributed to Aesop, and in circulation at the time of Heraclitus, a personified πόλεμος (as the δαίμων of kindred strife) married a personified ὕβρις (as the δαίμων of arrogant pride) [38] and that it was a common folk belief that πόλεμος accompanied ὕβρις - that is, that Polemos followed Hubris around rather than vice versa, causing or bringing ἔρις.

As a result of ἔρις, there often arises πάθει μάθος - that practical and personal knowing, that reasoned understanding which, according to Aeschylus [39] is the new law, the new understanding, given by Zeus to replace the older more religious and dogmatic way of fear and dread, often viewed as Μοῖραι τρίμορφοι μνήμονές τ' Ἐρινύες [40]. A new understanding which Aeschylus saught to explain in the Oresteia.

III - Being and Empathy

This understanding is basically that of a particular balance, born from πάθει μάθος (from the personal knowing of the error, the unbalance, that is ὕβρις) and from using reasoned judgement (σωφρονεῖν), and both of which make us aware of the true nature of our φύσις and of Φύσις itself.

In addition, by cultivating and by using our natural faculty of empathy, we can understand both φύσις and Πόλεμος, and thus apprehend Being as Being, and the nature of beings - and in particular the nature of our being, as mortals. For empathy reveals to us the acausality of Being [41] and thus how the process of abstraction, involving as it does an imposition of causality and separation upon beings (and the ideation implicit on opposites and dialectic), is a covering-up of Being and of Πόλεμος and thus involves a mis-understanding of both Δίκα and of φύσις.

In place of the numinosity of ψυχή - of Life qua being - there is, for the apprehension that is a dialectic of opposites, the hubris of abstractions, and thus a loss of our natural balance, a loss of ἁρμονίη [42] and συμπάθεια.

Appendix I

The Principle of Δίκα

Δίκα is that noble, respectful, balance understood, for example, by Sophocles (among many others) - for instance, Antigone respects the natural balance, the customs and traditions of her own culture, given by the gods, whereas Creon verges towards and finally commits, like Oedipus in Oedipus Tyrannus, the error of ὕβρις and is thus "taught a lesson" (just like Oedipus) by the gods because, as Aeschylus wrote -

Δίκα δὲ τοῖς μὲν παθοῦσ-
ιν μαθεῖν ἐπιρρέπει

The goddess, Judgement, favours someone learning from adversity.

Agamemnon, 250-251

In respect of Δίκα, I write - spell - it thus in this modern way with a capital Δ to intimate a new, a particular and numinous, philosophical principle, and differentiate it from the more general δίκη. As a numinous principle, or axiom, Δίκα thus suggests what lies beyond and what may have been the genesis of δίκη personified as the goddess, Judgement – the goddess of natural balance, of the ancestral way and ancestral customs.

Thus, Δίκα does not mean nor imply something theological, but rather implies the natural balance, the reasoned judgement, the thoughtful reasoning – σωφρονεῖν – that πάθει μάθος brings and restores, and which accumulated πάθει μάθος of a particular folk or πόλις forms the basis for their ancestral customs. δίκη is therefore, as the numinous principle Δίκα, what may be said to be a particular and a necessary balance between ἀρετή and ὕβρις - between the ὕβρις that often results when the personal, the natural, quest for ἀρετή becomes unbalanced and excessive.

That is, when ἔρις (discord) is or becomes δίκη – as suggested by Heraclitus in Fragment 80 -

εἰδέναι δὲ χρὴ τὸν πόλεμον ἐόντα ξυνόν, καὶ δίκην ἔριν, καὶ γινόμενα πάντα κατ᾽ ἔριν καὶ χρεώμενα [χρεών]

One should be aware that Polemos pervades, with discord δίκη, and that beings are naturally born by discord.

Appendix II

From Mythoi To Empathy
A New Appreciation Of The Numinous

Since the concept of the numinous is central to my weltanschauung - otherwise known as the 'philosophy of pathei-mathos' - it seems apposite to provide, as I did in respect of my use of the term physis, φύσις [1], a more detailed explanation of the concept, and my usage of it, than I have hitherto given, deriving as the term does from the classical Latin numen which denoted "a reverence for the divine; a divinity; divine power" with the word numen assimilated into English in the 15th century, with the English use of 'numinous' dating from the middle of the 17th century and used to signify "of or relating to a numen; revealing or indicating the presence of a divinity; divine, spiritual."

The term numinous was also used in a somewhat restrictive religious way [2] by Rudolf Otto over a century ago in his book *Das Heilige*.

In contrast to Otto et al, my understanding of the numinous is that it is primarily a perceiveration, not a personal emotion or feeling, not a mysterium, and not an idea in the sense of Plato's εἶδος and thus is not similar to Kant's concept of *a priori*. As a perceiveration, while it includes an apprehension of what is often referred to as 'the divine', 'the holy' - and sometimes thus is an apprehension of theos or theoi - it is not limited to such apprehensions, since as in the past it is often an intimation of, an intuition concerning,

> "the natural balance of ψυχή; a balance which ὕβρις upsets. This natural balance – our being as human beings – is or can be manifest to us in or by what is harmonious, or what reminds us of what is harmonious and beautiful." [3]

Where ψυχή is an intimation of, an intuition concerning Life *qua* being; of ourselves as a living existent considered as an emanation of ψυχή, howsoever ψυχή is described, as for example in mythoi - and thus in terms of theos, theoi, or 'Nature' - with ψυχή thus what 'animates' us and what gives us our φύσις as human beings. A physis classically perceived to be that of a mortal fallible being

veering between σωφρονεῖν (thoughtful reasoning, and thus fairness) and ὕβρις.
[4]

The particular apprehension of external reality that is the numinous is that provided by our natural faculty of empathy, ἐμπάθεια. When this particular faculty is developed and used then it is a specific and extended type of συμπάθεια. That is, it is a type of and a means to knowing and understanding another human being and/or other living beings. The type of 'knowing' - and thence the understanding - that empathy provides or can provide is different from, but supplementary and complimentary to, that knowing which may be acquired by means of the Aristotelian essentials of conventional philosophy and experimental science.

Furthermore, since empathy is a natural and an individual human faculty, it

> "is limited in range and application, just as our faculties of sight and hearing are limited in range and application. These limits extend to only what is direct, immediate, and involve personal interactions with other humans or with other living beings. There is therefore, for the philosophy of pathei-mathos, an 'empathic scale of things' and an acceptance of our limitations of personal knowing and personal understanding." [5]

That is, as I explained in my 2015 essay *Personal Reflexions On Some Metaphysical Questions*, there is a 'local horizon of empathy'.

This local horizon and the fact that empathy is a human faculty mean that the apprehension is wordless and personal and cannot be extrapolated beyond, or abstracted out from, the individual without losing some or all of its numinosity since the process of denotatum - of abstraction - devolves around the meanings assigned to words, terms, and names, and which meanings can and do vary over causal time and may be (mis)interpreted by others often on the basis of some idea, or theory, or on some comparative exegesis.

It therefore follows that the numinous cannot be codified and that numinosity cannot be adequately, fully, presenced by anything doctrinal or which is organized beyond a small, a localized, and thus personal level; and that all such a supra-local organization can ever hope to do at best is provide a fallible intimation of the numinous, or perhaps some practical means to help others toward individually apprehending the numinous for themselves.

Which intimation, given the nature of empathy - with its συμπάθεια, with its wordless knowing of actually being for a moment or for moments 'the living other' - is of muliebral virtues such as compassion, manners, and a certain personal humility, and of how a shared, mutual, personal love can and does presence the numinous. Which intimation, which wisdom, which knowing, is exactly that of our thousands of years old human culture of pathei-mathos, and which culture - with its personal recounting, and artistic renderings, of tragedy, love, loss, suffering, and war - is a far better guide to the numinous than conventional religions. [6]

All of which is why I wrote in my *Tu Es Diaboli Ianua* that in my view "the numinous is primarily a manifestation of the muliebral," and that revealed religions such as Christianity, Islam, and Judaism primarily manifest a presencing of the masculous. Such religions - indeed all religions - therefore have not presenced, and do not and cannot presence, the numinous as the numinous can be presenced. Neither did Greco-Roman culture, for all its assimilation of some muliebral mythoi, adequately presence the numinous, and just as no modern organized paganus revival dependant on mythoi and anthropomorphic deities can adequately presence the numinous.

For the cultivation of the faculty of empathy is the transition from mythoi and anthropomorphic deities (theos and theoi) to an appreciation of the numinous sans denotatum and sans religion.

A New Appreciation Of The Numinous

How then can the faculty of empathy be cultivated? My own practical experience of various religions, as well as my own pathei-mathos, inclines me to favour the personal cultivation of muliebral virtues and a return to a more local, a less organized, way or ways of living based initially on a personal and mutual and loyal love between two individuals. A living of necessity balanced by personal honour given how the world is still replete with dishonourable hubriatic individuals who, devoid of empathy, are often motivated by the worst of intentions. For such a personal honour - in the immediacy of the personal moment - is a necessary restoration of the numinous balance that the dishonourable deeds of a hubriatic individual or individuals upsets [7].

For such a personal love, such a preparedness to restore the natural balance through honour, are - in my admittedly fallible view - far more adequate presencings of the numinous than any religious ritual, than any religious worship, or any type of contemplative (wordless) prayer.

David Myatt
January 2018

[1] *Toward Understanding Physis*. Included in the 2015 compilation *Sarigthersa*.

[2] I have endeavoured in recent years to make a distinction between a religion and a spiritual 'way of life'. As noted in Appendix VII - Glossary of The Philosophy of Pathei-Mathos, *Religion,*

"One of the differences being that a religion requires and manifests a codified ritual and doctrine and a certain expectation of conformity in terms of doctrine and ritual, as well as a certain organization beyond the local community level resulting in particular individuals assuming or being appointed to positions of authority in matters relating to that religion. In contrast, Ways are more diverse and more an expression of a spiritual ethos, of a customary, and often localized, way of doing certain spiritual things, with there generally being little or no organization beyond the community level and no individuals assuming - or being appointed by some organization - to positions of authority in matters relating to that ethos.

Religions thus tend to develope an organized regulatory and supra-local hierarchy which oversees and appoints those, such as priests or religious teachers, regarded as proficient in spiritual matters and in matters of doctrine and ritual, whereas adherents of Ways tend to locally and informally and communally, and out of respect and a personal knowing, accept certain individuals as having a detailed knowledge and an understanding of the ethos and the practices of that Way. Many spiritual Ways have evolved into religions."

Another difference is that religions tend to presence and be biased toward the masculous, while spiritual ways tend to be either more muliebral or incorporate muliebral virtues.

[3] Myatt, David. *The Numinous Way of Pathei-Mathos*, 2103. Appendix VII - Glossary of The Philosophy of Pathei-Mathos, *The Numinous*.

[4] In my note *Concerning σωφρονεῖν* - included in my "revised 2455621.531" version of *The Balance of Physis – Notes on λόγος and ἀληθέα in Heraclitus. Part One, Fragment 112* - I mentioned that I use σωφρονεῖν (sophronein) in preference to σωφροσύνη (sophrosyne) since sophrosyne has acquired an English interpretation – "soundness of mind, moderation" – which in my view distorts the meaning of the original Greek. As with my use of the term πάθει μάθος (pathei-mathos) I use σωφρονεῖν in an Anglicized manner with there thus being no necessity to employ inflective forms.

[5] Qv. Appendix VII - *Immediacy-of-the-Moment*.

[6] One aspect of the apprehension of the numinous that empathy provides - which I have briefly touched upon in various recent personal writings - is that personal love is personal love; personal, mutual, equal, and germane to the moment and to a person. It thus does not adhere to manufactured or assumed abstractive boundaries such as gender, social status, or nationality, with enforced adherence to such presumptive boundaries - such as opposition to same gender love whether from religious or political beliefs - contrary to

empathy and a cause of suffering.

[7] As mentioned in my *The Numinous Way of Pathei-Mathos*,

> "The personal virtue of honour, and the cultivation of wu-wei, are –
> together – a practical, a living, manifestation of our understanding
> and appreciation of the numinous; of how to live, to behave, as
> empathy intimates we can or should in order to avoid committing the
> folly, the error, of ὕβρις, in order not to cause suffering, and in order
> to re-present, to acquire, ἀρμονίη.
>
> For personal honour is essentially a presencing, a grounding, of ψυχή
> – of Life, of our φύσις – occurring when the insight (the knowing) of a
> developed empathy inclines us toward a compassion that is, of
> necessity, balanced by σωφρονεῖν and in accord with δίκη.
>
> This balancing of compassion – of the need not to cause suffering – by
> σωφρονεῖν and δίκη is perhaps most obvious on that particular
> occasion when it may be judged necessary to cause suffering to
> another human being. That is, in honourable self-defence. For it is
> natural – part of our reasoned, fair, just, human nature – to defend
> ourselves when attacked and (in the immediacy of the personal
> moment) to valorously, with chivalry, act in defence of someone
> close-by who is unfairly attacked or dishonourably threatened or is
> being bullied by others, and to thus employ, if our personal judgement
> of the circumstances deem it necessary, lethal force.
>
> This use of force is, importantly, crucially, restricted – by the
> individual nature of our judgement, and by the individual nature of
> our authority – to such personal situations of immediate self-defence
> and of valorous defence of others, and cannot be extended beyond
> that, for to so extend it, or attempt to extend it beyond the immediacy
> of the personal moment of an existing physical threat, is an arrogant
> presumption – an act of ὕβρις – which negates the fair, the human,
> presumption of innocence of those we do not personally know, we
> have no empathic knowledge of, and who present no direct,
> immediate, personal, threat to us or to others nearby us.
>
> Such personal self-defence and such valorous defence of another in a
> personal situation are in effect a means to restore the natural balance
> which the unfair, the dishonourable, behaviour of others upsets. That
> is, such defence fairly, justly, and naturally in the immediacy of the
> moment corrects their error of ὕβρις resulting from their bad (their
> rotten) φύσις; a rotten character evident in their lack of the virtue,
> the skill, of σωφρονεῖν. For had they possessed that virtue, and if their
> character was not bad, they would not have undertaken such a
> dishonourable attack."

Appendix III

Towards Understanding Ancestral Culture

As manifest in my weltanschauung, based as that weltanschauung is on pathei-mathos and an appreciation of Greco-Roman culture, the term Ancestral Culture is synonymous with Ancestral Custom, with Ancestral Custom represented in Ancient Greek mythoi by Δίκη, the goddess Fairness as described by Hesiod:

> σὺ δ᾽ ἄκουε δίκης, μηδ᾽ ὕβριν ὄφελλε:
> ὕβρις γάρ τε κακὴ δειλῷ βροτῷ: οὐδὲ μὲν ἐσθλὸς
> 215 ῥηιδίως φερέμεν δύναται, βαρύθει δέ θ᾽ ὑπ᾽ αὐτῆς
> ἐγκύρσας ἄτῃσιν: ὁδὸς δ᾽ ἑτέρηφι παρελθεῖν
> κρείσσων ἐς τὰ δίκαια: Δίκη δ᾽ ὑπὲρ Ὕβριος ἴσχει
> ἐς τέλος ἐξελθοῦσα: παθὼν δέ τε νήπιος ἔγνω

> You should listen to Fairness and not oblige Hubris
> Since Hubris harms unfortunate mortals while even the more fortunate
> Are not equal to carrying that heavy a burden, meeting as they do with Mischief.
> The best path to take is the opposite one: that of honour
> For, in the end, Fairness is above Hubris
> Which is something the young come to learn from adversity.

> Hesiod, Ἔργα καὶ Ἡμέραι [Works and Days], vv 213-218

That Δίκη is generally described as the goddess of 'justice' - as 'Judgement' personified - is unfortunate given that the terms 'justice' and 'judgement' have modern, abstract, and legalistic, connotations which are inappropriate and which detract from understanding and appreciating the mythoi of Ancient Greece and Rome.

Correctly understood, Δίκη - and δίκη in general - represents the natural and the necessary balance manifest in ἁρμονίη (harmony) and thus not only in τὸ καλόν (the beautiful) but also in the Cosmic Order, κόσμος, with ourselves as human beings (at least when unaffected by hubris) a microcosmic re-presentation of such balance, κόσμον δὲ θείου σώματος κατέπεμψε τὸν ἄνθρωπον [1]. A sentiment re-expressed centuries later by Marsilii Ficini:

> Quomodo per inferiora superioribus exposita deducantur superiora, et per mundanas materias mundana potissimum dona.

> How, when what is lower is touched by what is higher, the higher is cosmically presenced therein and thus gifted because cosmically aligned. [2]

This understanding and appreciation of ἁρμονίη and of κόσμος and of ourselves as a microcosm is perhaps most evident in the Greek phrase καλὸς κἀγαθός, describing as it does those who are balanced within themselves, who - manifesting τὸ καλόν and τὸ ἀγαθὸν - comport themselves in a gentlemanly or lady-like manner, part of which comportment is living and if necessary dying in a honourable, a noble, manner. For personal honour presences τὸ καλόν and τὸ ἀγαθὸν, and thus the numinous.

For in practice honour manifests the customary, the ancestral way, of those who are noble, those who presence fairness; those who restore balance; those who (even at some cost to themselves) are fair due to their innate physis or because they have been nurtured to be so. For this ancestral way - such ancestral custom - is what is expected in terms of personal behaviour based on past personal examples and thus often manifests the accumulated wisdom of previous generations.

Thus, an important - perhaps even ethos-defining - Ancestral Custom of Greco-Roman culture, and of Western culture born as Western culture was from medieval mythoi involving Knights and courtly romance and from the re-discovery of Greco-Roman culture that began the Renaissance, is chivalry and which personal virtue - presencing the numinous as it does and did - is not and cannot be subject to any qualifications or exceptions and cannot be confined to or manifest by anything so supra-personal as a particular religion or anything so supra-personal as a political dogma or ideology.

Hence, the modern paganus weltanschauung that I mentioned in my *Classical Paganism And The Christian Ethos* as a means "to reconnect those in the lands of the West, and those in Western émigré lands and former colonies of the West, with their ancestral ethos," is one founded on καλὸς κἀγαθός. That is, on chivalry; on manners; on gentrice romance; and on the muliebral virtues, the gender equality, inherent in both chivalry and personal manners, consciously and rationally understood as chivalry and manners now are as a consequence of both our thousands of years old human culture of pathei-mathos and of our empathic (wordless) and personal apprehension of the numinous.

David Myatt
January 2018

[1] "a cosmos of the divine body sent down as human beings." Tractate IV:2. Corpus Hermeticum. Ἑρμοῦ πρὸς Τάτ ὁ κρατῆρ ἡ μονάς.

[2] De Vita Coelitus Comparanda. XXVI.

Appendix IV

The Concept Of Physis

The term physis - φύσις - was used by Heraclitus, Aristotle, and others, and occurs in texts such as the Pœmandres and Ιερός Λόγος tractates of the Corpus Hermeticum.

Physis is usually translated as either 'Nature' (as if 'the natural world', and the physical cosmos beyond, are meant) or as the character (the nature) of a person. However, while the context - of the original Greek text - may suggest (as often, for example, in Homer and Herodotus) such a meaning as such English words impute, physis philosophically (as, for example, in Heraclitus and Aristotle and the Corpus Hermeticum) has specific ontological meanings. Meanings which are lost, or glossed over, when physis is simply translated either as 'Nature' or - in terms of mortals - as (personal) character.

Ontologically, as Aristotle makes clear [2], physis denotes the being of those beings who or which have the potentiality (the being) to change, be changed, or to develope. That is, to become, or to move or be moved; as for example in the motion (of 'things') and the 'natural unfolding' or growth, sans an external cause, that living beings demonstrate.

However, and crucially, physis is not - for human beings - some abstract 'essence' (qv. Plato's ἰδέα/εἶδος) but rather a balance between the being that it is, it was, and potentially might yet be. That is, in Aristotelian terms, it is a meson - μέσον - of being and 'not being'; and 'not being' in the sense of not yet having become what it could be, and not now being what it used to be. Hence why, for Aristotle, a manifestation of physis - in terms of the being of mortals - such as arête (ἀρετή) is a meson, a balance of things, and not, as it is for Plato, some fixed 'form' - some idea, ideal - which as Plato wrote "always exists, and has no genesis. It does not die, does not grow, does not decay." [3]

According to my understanding of Heraclitus, physis also suggests - as in Fragment 1 - the 'natural' being of a being which we mortals have a tendency to cover-up or conceal [4].

Furthermore, physis is one of the main themes in the Pœmandres tractate of the Corpus Hermeticum, for the author seeks "to apprehend the physis of beings" [5] with physis often mystically personified:

> "This is a mysterium esoteric even to this day. For Physis, having intimately joined with the human, produced a most wondrous wonder possessed of the physis of the harmonious seven I mentioned before, of Fire and pneuma. Physis did not tarry, giving birth to seven male-and-female humans with the physis of those viziers, and

ætherean...

[For] those seven came into being in this way. Earth was muliebral, Water was lustful, and Fire maturing. From Æther, the pnuema, and with Physis bringing forth human-shaped bodies. Of Life and phaos, the human came to be of psyche and perceiveration; from Life - psyche; from phaos - perceiveration; and with everything in the observable cosmic order cyclic until its completion...

When the cycle was fulfilled, the connexions between all things were, by the deliberations of theos, unfastened. Living beings - all male-and-female then - were, including humans, rent asunder thus bringing into being portions that were masculous with the others muliebral." [6]

Physis is also personified in the Ιερός Λόγος tractate:

"The divine is all of that mixion: renewance of the cosmic order through Physis For Physis is presenced in the divine." [7]

The Numinous Way Of Pathei-Mathos

In the philosophy of pathei-mathos, physis is used contextually to refer to:

(i) the ontology of beings, an ontology - a reality, a 'true nature '- that is often obscured by denotatum [9] and by abstractions, both of which conceal physis;
(ii) the relationship between beings, and between beings and Being, which is of us - we mortals - as a nexion, an affective effluvium (or emanation) of Life (ψυχή) and thus of why 'the separation-of-otherness' is a concealment of that relationship;
(iii) the character, or persona, of human beings, and which character - sans denotatum - can be discovered (revealed, known) by the faculty of empathy;
(iv) the unity - the being - beyond the division of our physis, as individual mortals, into masculous and muliebral;
(v) that manifestation denoted by the concept Time, with Time considered to be an expression/manifestation of the physis of beings.

My concept of physis is therefore primarily ontological.

David Myatt
March 2015

Notes

[1] I have included here ,as Appendix IV, my translation of, and notes on, the relevant part of 1015α.

[2] See Appendix IV, below, and also my *Personal Reflexions On Some Metaphysical Questions*.

[3] πρῶτον μὲν ἀεὶ ὂν καὶ οὔτε γιγνόμενον οὔτε ἀπολλύμενον οὔτε αὐξανόμενον οὔτε φθίνον (Symposium 210e - 211a).

[4] See Appendix V.

[5] Pœmandres 3; qv. my *Mercvrii Trismegisti Pymander de potestate et sapientia dei: A Translation and Commentary*, 2013.

[6] Pœmandres 16-18.

[7] Ιερός Λόγος 3; qv. my *Ιερός Λόγος: An Esoteric Mythos. A Translation Of And A Commentary On The Third Tractate Of The Corpus Hermeticum*, 2015.

[9] In my philosophy of pathei-mathos, I use the term denotatum - from the Latin, denotare - in accord with its general meaning which is "to denote or to describe by an expression or a word; to name some-thing; to refer that which is so named or so denoted."

[10] An abstraction is a manufactured generalization, a hypothesis, a posited thing, an assumption or assumptions about, an extrapolation of or from some-thing, or some assumed or extrapolated ideal 'form' of some-thing. Sometimes, abstractions are generalization based on some sample(s), or on some median (average) value or sets of values, observed, sampled, or assumed.

Abstractions can be of some-thing past, in the present, or described as a goal or an ideal which it is assumed could be attained or achieved in the future. Abstractions are often assumed to provide some 'knowledge' or some 'understanding' of some-thing assigned to or described by a particular abstraction.

[11] Refer, for example, to my *The Error of The-Separation-of-Otherness* in *The Numinous Way of Pathei-Mathos*, 2012.

[12] *Time And The Separation Of Otherness - Part One.* 2012.

Text

ἐκ δὴ τῶν εἰρημένων ἡ πρώτη φύσις καὶ κυρίως λεγομένη ἐστὶν ἡ οὐσία ἡ τῶν ἐχόντων ἀρχὴν κινήσεως ἐν αὐτοῖς ἦ αὐτά: ἡ γὰρ ὕλη τῷ ταύτης δεκτικὴ εἶναι λέγεται φύσις, καὶ αἱ γενέσεις καὶ τὸ φύεσθαι τῷ ἀπὸ ταύτης εἶναι κινήσεις. καὶ ἡ ἀρχὴ τῆς κινήσεως τῶν φύσει ὄντων αὕτη ἐστίν, ἐνυπάρχουσά πως ἢ δυνάμει ἢ ἐντελεχείᾳ.

Translation

Given the foregoing, then principally - and to be exact - physis denotes the quidditas of beings having changement inherent within them; for substantia has been denoted by physis because it embodies this, as have the becoming that is a coming-into-being, and a burgeoning, because they are changements predicated on it. For physis is inherent changement either manifesting the potentiality of a being or as what a being, complete of itself, is.

Commentary And Notes

physis. φύσις. A transliteration, since (i) this is a fundamental philosophical principle/term that requires contextual interpretation, and (ii) the English words 'nature' and Nature not only do not adequately describe this principle but also lead to and have led to certain misunderstandings of Aristotle in particular and of classical Greek culture in general.

quidditas. οὐσία. Quidditas - post-classical Latin, from whence the English word 'quiddity' - is more appropriate here than 'essence', given the metaphysical (ontological) context and given that 'essence' now has so many non-philosophical connotations. An interesting alternative would be the scholastic term haeceitty. As with physis, quidditas is a philosophical term which requires contextual interpretation.

changement inherent. The expression ἀρχὴν κινήσεως is crucial to understanding what Aristotle means in respect of physis. In regard to κίνησις, since Aristotle here does not mean 'motion' or 'movement' in the sense of Newtonian physics (with its causal concepts of force, mass, velocity, kinetic energy), and since such physical movement is what the English words 'motion' and 'movement' now most usually denote, then alternatives must be found. Hence the translation 'changement'.

For what Aristotle is describing here is 'change', as for example in the natural development, the unfolding, the growth, of some-thing living that occurs because it is living; because it is possessed of Life and which Life is the ἀρχή of the changement, the 'original being' (the φύσις) from whence being-becomes to be often perceived and classified by us in orderly ways.

What is described is an a-causal change, of being-becoming - of being unfolding - and thus fulfilling the potentiality of being within it. Hence why here Aristotle writes ἀρχὴν κινήσεως, which describes the potential changement inherent in certain beings. [1] That is, the a-causal origin of beings-becoming, or having become, and which beings (having changed, developed, unfolded) we then perceive and classify in orderly ways [2], such as by shape or usefulness to us, or by a notion such as causality: in terms of physical- 'movement'. Which is why, in Aristotle, there is a relation between φύσις, μορφή, and εἶδος - εἶδος in the sense of 'perceiveration' and not, as in Plato, denoting an abstract 'form' or an 'ideal' - διὸ καὶ ὅσα φύσει ἔστιν ἢ γίγνεται, ἤδη ὑπάρχοντος ἐξ οὗ πέφυκε γίγνεσθαι ἢ εἶναι, οὔπω φαμὲν τὴν φύσιν ἔχειν ἐὰν μὴ ἔχῃ τὸ εἶδος καὶ τὴν μορφήν.

Thus φύσις is what is a-causal in beings and which acausality is the origin of the 'natural' order that unfolds because of the potentiality of being to become, to presence in the causal, whence to be perceived by us in various orderly arrangements and/or arranged in terms of usefulness, and which arrangements/usefulness include τὸ καλόν - and thus schemata, τάξις [3] - and ἀρετή.

substantia. ὕλη. I have chosen to use the etymon of the English word 'substance' - qv. substantia in Thomas Aquinas, *Sententia libri Metaphysicae* - to again (i) emphasize the need for contextual interpretation in respect of a specific philosophical term, and (ii) to avoid whatever misunderstandings may arise from the modern (non-ontological) connotations of words such as 'matter' and 'substance'.

as have the becoming that is a coming-into-being, and a burgeoning, because they are changements predicated on it. καὶ αἱ γενέσεις καὶ τὸ φύεσθαι τῷ ἀπὸ ταύτης εἶναι κινήσεις. The sense of γένεσις here implies a 'coming-into-being' rather than just 'generation', just as φύω implies a being 'burgeoning' - unfolding, revealing itself (its physis) - rather than just 'growing'.

the potentiality of a being or as what a being, complete of itself, is. The Greek word ἐντελεχεία is compounded from ἐν ἐλει ἔχει and the sense here - in relation to ἐνυπάρχουσά - seems to be twofold: of a being as an unchanged being, and of what a being has become (or is becoming) as a result of a change, for both types of being actually exist, are real. One exists as a being as it is and has remained, and one exists as the being it has become (or is in the process of becoming) through the potential for changement inherent within it. Thus, for Aristotle, physis denotes the being of both types of being.

DWM
March 2015

[1] In respect of ἀρχὴ as implying what is primarily inherent, qv. 1012b-1013a.

[2] As Thomas Aquinas wrote: "Sciendum est autem, quod principium et causa licet sint idem subiecto, differunt tamen ratione. Nam hoc nomen principium ordinem quemdam importat; hoc vero nomen causa, importat influxum quemdam ad esse causati." *Sententia libri Metaphysicae*, liber 5, lectio 1, n 3.

[3] Regarding 1078a, τοῦ δὲ καλοῦ μέγιστα εἴδη τάξις καὶ συμμετρία καὶ τὸ ὡρισμένον (the most noticeable expressions of kalos are schemata and harmony and consonancy), my view - given the context - is that τάξις here is best translated as "schemata", rather than "order" or "arrangement" both of which are vague, open to mis-interpretation, and unrelated to the context, which context is mathematical beauty. Similarly, ὁρίζω (to me) suggests consonancy, echoing as that (now somewhat obscure) English word does both by its use by, among others, Shakespeare (Hamlet, Act 2, Scene 2, 286) and also by its relation to the almost 'mathematical beauty' of some music (as evident for example in the counterpoint of JS Bach).

Furthermore, just because the Greek has συμμετρία it does not necessarily follow that the English word 'symmetry' is an appropriate translation, considering how the word symmetry is now used and has been used, in the West for many centuries, and especially in relation to art (in terms, for example, of objects and the human body).

Given that Aristotle in 1078a is referring to geometry in particular and mathematics in general, then an appropriate translation is 'harmony' - as in "a collation of representative signs or marks, so arranged that they exhibit their agreement and account for their discrepancies or errors." A harmony, in other words, that is most evident (as I mentioned in my essay) in Euclid's Elements, as schemata and consonancy are therein evident, most of the contents (theorems) of which book - deriving from people such as Pythagoras - were known to Aristotle.

Thus, a translation such as "the chief forms of beauty are order and symmetry and definiteness" can in my opinion lead to projecting onto Aristotle what he may not necessarily have meant; and projecting onto in respect of how we now, over two thousand years after Aristotle, understand and use such common English terms. Hence, also, why I sometimes use obscure English words (which may suggest a relevant meaning) or transliterations (as in physis).

Appendix VI

Some Notes on Heraclitus Fragment 1

Text

τοῦ δὲ λόγου τοῦδ᾽ ἐόντος ἀεὶ ἀξύνετοι γίνονται ἄνθρωποι καὶ
πρόσθεν ἢ ἀκοῦσαι καὶ ἀκούσαντες τὸ πρῶτον· γινομένων γὰρ
πάντων κατὰ τὸν λόγον τόνδε ἀπείροισιν ἐοίκασι, πειρώμενοι καὶ
ἐπέων καὶ ἔργων τοιούτων, ὁκοίων ἐγὼ διηγεῦμαι κατὰ φύσιν
διαιρέων ἕκαστον καὶ φράζων ὅκως ἔχει· τοὺς δὲ ἄλλους ἀνθρώπους
λανθάνει ὁκόσα ἐγερθέντες ποιοῦσιν, ὅκωσπερ ὁκόσα εὕδοντες
ἐπιλανθάνονται

Translation

My translation of the fragment is:

> Although this naming and expression [which I explain] exists, human
> beings tend to ignore it, both before and after they have become
> aware of it. Yet even though, regarding such naming and expression, I
> have revealed details of how Physis has been cleaved asunder, some
> human beings are inexperienced concerning it, fumbling about with
> words and deeds, just as other human beings, be they interested or
> just forgetful, are unaware of what they have done.

Comments

1. λόγος

In respect of fragments 80 and 112 I have suggested that it is incorrect to
interpret πόλεμος simplistically as 'war', strife, or kampf [1] and that, instead of
using such words, it should be transliterated so as to name a distinct
philosophical principle that requires interpretation and explanation with
particular reference to Hellenic culture and philosophy. For, more often than
not, such common English words as 'war' are now understood in a non-Hellenic,
non-philosophical, context and explained in relation to some ideated opposite;
and in the particular case of the term 'war', for example, in contrast to
some-thing named, explained, or defined, as 'peace' or a state of
non-belligerence.

In respect of fragment 1 [2], does λόγος suggest a philosophical principle and
therefore should it, like πόλεμος, be transliterated and thus be considered as a
basic principle of the philosophy of Heraclitus, or at least of what, of that

philosophy or weltanschauung, we can adduce from the textual fragments we possess? Or does λόγος, as I suggested in respect of fragment 112 and 123 [3] imply:

> both *a naming* (denoting), and *a telling* – not a telling as in some abstract explanation or theory, but as in a simple describing, or recounting, of what has been so denoted or so named. Which is why, in fragment 39, Heraclitus writes:

> > ἐν Πριήνηι Βίας ἐγένετο ὁ Τευτάμεω, οὗ πλείων λόγος ἢ
> > τῶν ἄλλων [4]

> and why, in respect of λέγειν, Hesiod wrote:

> > ἴδμεν ψεύδεα πολλὰ λέγειν ἐτύμοισιν ὁμοῖα,
> > ἴδμεν δ᾽, εὖτ᾽ ἐθέλωμεν, ἀληθέα γηρύσασθαι [5]

I contend that fragment 1 also suggests a denoting, in the sense of expressing some-thing by denoting it or describing it by a 'name'. That is, that λόγος here does not refer here to what has often be termed Logos, and that the 'ambiguous' ἀεὶ [6] is not really ambiguous at all.

For one has to, in my view, take account of the fact that there is poetry in Heraclitus; a rather underrated style that sometimes led others to incorrectly describe him as ὁ σκοτεινός, the ambiguous (or the obtuse) one, and led Aristotle to write:

> τὰ γὰρ Ἡρακλείτου διαστίξαι ἔργον διὰ τὸ ἄδηλον
> εἶναι ποτέρῳ πρόσκειται, τῷ ὕστερον ἢ τῷ πρότερον, οἷον ἐν τῇ ἀρχῇ
> αὐτῇ τοῦ συγγράμματος:
> φησὶ γὰρ "τοῦ λόγου τοῦδ᾽ ἐόντος ἀεὶ ἀξύνετοι ἄνθρωποι γίγνονται":
> ἄδηλον γὰρ τὸ ἀεί, πρὸς ποτέρῳ δεῖ διαστίξαι. [6]

It is the poetic style of Heraclitus that I have tried, however badly, to express in my often non-literal and rather idiosyncratic translations/interpretations of some of the fragments attributed to him. Hence my interpretation of the first part:

> Although this naming and expression [which I explain] exists – human beings tend to ignore it, both before and after they have become aware of it.

The 'which I explain' being implicit in the sense of λόγος here as a naming and expression by a particular individual, contrasted (as often with Heraclitus) rather poetically with a generality; in this instance, contrasted with human beings - 'men' - in general.

2. ἀεὶ

In my view, "tend to" captures the poetic sense of ἀεὶ here. That is, the literal - the bland, strident - 'always' is discarded in favour of a more Heraclitean expression of human beings having an apparently rather irreconcilable tendency - both now and as in the past - to ignore (or forget or not understand) certain things, even after matters have been explained to them (they have heard the explanation) and even after they have discovered certain truths for themselves.

3. διαιρέων and Φύσις

I take the sense of διαιρέων here somewhat poetically to suggest not the ordinary 'divide' but the more expressive 'cleave', with it being undivided Physis that is cleaved into parts by "such naming and expression" as Heraclitus has revealed. That is, Heraclitus is not saying that he has described or expressed each thing 'in accordance with its true nature' (or divided things correctly, or something of the kind) but rather that the process of naming and categorization is or has divided Physis, obscuring the true nature of Being and beings, and it is this process, this obscuring, or concealment. of Physis - of cleaving it into separate parts or each thing, 'each' contrasted with a generality [7] - that he has revealed and is mentioning here, as he mentioned it in fragment 123:

Φύσις κρύπτεσθαι φιλεῖ

Concealment accompanies Physis [8]

Which is why I have transliterated Φύσις as referring to a general philosophical principle of the philosophy of Heraclitus, or at least of what, of that philosophy or weltanschauung, we can adduce from the textual fragments we possess.

4. πειρώμενοι καὶ ἐπέων καὶ ἔργων τοιούτων

In respect of ἐπέων καὶ ἔργων τοιούτων, the Homeric usage [9] is, for me, interesting as it implies a proverbial kind of saying rather than just 'words' and 'deeds':

Τηλέμαχ᾽, οὐδ᾽ ὄπιθεν κακὸς ἔσσεαι οὐδ᾽ ἀνοήμων,
εἰ δή τοι σοῦ πατρὸς ἐνέστακται μένος ἠύ,
οἷος κεῖνος ἔην τελέσαι ἔργον τε ἔπος τε:

Telemachus – you will not be unlucky nor lacking in resolution
If you hereafter instill into yourself the determination of your father

Whose nature was to accomplish those deeds he said he would.

Furthermore, I take the sense here of πειρώμενοι poetically to suggest a "fumbling about" - as the inexperienced often fumble about and experiment until, often by trial and error, they have gained sufficient experience to understand and know what they are doing and what is involved, which rather reminds one of a saying of Pindar [10]:

γλυκὺ δὲ πόλεμος ἀπείροισιν, ἐμπείρων δέ τις
ταρβεῖ προσιόντα νιν καρδίᾳ περισσῶ

5. ἐγερθέντες and εὔδοντες

Given that, as mentioned above, there is poetry in Heraclitus, I am inclined to avoid the literal, and usual, understanding of ἐγερθέντες and εὔδοντες, particularly given the foregoing πειρώμενοι καὶ ἐπέων καὶ ἔργων τοιούτων which renders such a literal understanding not only out of context and disjointed but decidedly odd. Human beings forgetting things when they sleep? If, however, and for example, ἐγείρω here poetically suggests alertness, an interest or excitement - as ἤγειρεν in the Agamemnon suggests an alertness and excitement, an interest in what has occurred, and thence the kindling of a pyre [11] - then there is, as often in Heraclitus, a flowing eloquence and that lack of discordance one might expect of an aphorism remembered and recorded long after the demise of its author.

DWM
2013

Notes

[1] qv. *The Abstraction of Change as Opposites and Dialectic*, and *Some Notes on Πόλεμος and Δίκη in Heraclitus B80*

As mentioned in *The Abstraction of Change as Opposites and Dialectic:*

> "In addition, Polemos was originally the δαίμων [not the god] of kindred strife, whether familial, or of one's πόλις (one's clan and their places of dwelling). Thus, to describe Polemos, as is sometimes done, as the god of conflict (or war), is doubly incorrect."

[2] qv. Sextus Empiricus: *Advenus Mathematicos* VII. 132

[3] Regarding 123 - *Φύσις κρύπτεσθαι φιλεῖ* - qv. *Physis, Nature, Concealment, and Natural Change*, e-text 2010

[4] "In Priene was born someone named and recalled as most worthy – Bias, that son of Teutamas."

[5]

> We have many ways to conceal – to name – certain things
> And the skill when we wish to expose their meaning

[6] Aristotle: *Ars Rhetorica* Book 3, chapter 5 [1407b]

[7] As in Homer et al, for example Iliad, Book VII, 215 -

> Τρῶας δὲ τρόμος αἰνὸς ὑπήλυθε γυῖα ἕκαστον

> But over the Trojans, a strange fear, to shake the limbs of each one there

[8] qv. my *Physis, Nature, Concealment, and Natural Change* [Notes on Heraclitus fragment 123], e-text 2010

[9] Odyssey, Book II, 272

[10] Fragment 110

[11] Aeschylus, Agamemnon, 296-299

> σθένουσα λαμπὰς δ᾽ οὐδέπω μαυρουμένη,
> ὑπερθοροῦσα πεδίον Ἀσωποῦ, δίκην
> φαιδρᾶς σελήνης, πρὸς Κιθαιρῶνος λέπας
> ἤγειρεν ἄλλην ἐκδοχὴν πομποῦ πυρός.

> The torch, vigorous and far from extinguished,
> Bounded over the Asopian plain
> To the rocks of Cithaeron as bright as the moon
> So that the one waiting there to begin that fire, jumped up

Note that here the watchman is not awakened from sleep.

Glossary of The Philosophy of Pathei-Mathos
Vocabulary, Definitions, and Explanations

Abstraction

An abstraction is a manufactured generalization, a hypothesis, a posited thing, an assumption or assumptions about, an extrapolation of or from some-thing, or some assumed or extrapolated ideal 'form' of some-thing. Sometimes, abstractions are generalization based on some sample(s), or on some median (average) value or sets of values, observed, sampled, or assumed.

Abstractions can be of some-thing past, in the present, or described as a goal or an ideal which it is assumed could be attained or achieved in the future.

All abstractions involve a causal perception, based as they are on the presumption of a linear cause-and-effect (and/or a dialectic) and on a posited or an assumed category or classification which differs in some way from some other assumed or posited categories/classifications, past, present or future. When applied to or used to describe/classify/distinguish/motivate living beings, abstractions involve a causal separation-of-otherness; and when worth/value /identity (and exclusion/inclusion) is or are assigned to such a causal separation-of-otherness then there is or there arises hubris.

Abstractions are often assumed to provide some 'knowledge' or some 'understanding' of some-thing assigned to or described by a particular abstraction. For example, in respect of the abstraction of 'race' applied to human beings, and which categorization of human beings describes a median set of values said or assumed to exist 'now' or in some recent historical past.

According to the philosophy of pathei-mathos, this presumption of knowledge and understanding by the application of abstractions to beings - living and otherwise - is false, for abstractions are considered as a primary means by which the nature of Being and beings are and have been concealed, requiring as abstractions do the positing and the continuation of abstractive opposites in relation to Being and the separation of beings from Being by the process of ideation and opposites.

Acausal

The acausal is not a generalization – a concept – deriving from a collocation of assumed, imagined, or causally observed Phainómenon, but instead is that wordless, conceptless, a-temporal, knowing which empathy reveals and which a personal πάθει μάθος and an appreciation of the numinous often inclines us toward. That is, the acausal is a direct and personal (individual) revealing of beings and Being which does not depend on denoting or naming.

What is so revealed is the a-causal nature of some beings, the connexion which exists between living beings, and how living beings are emanations of ψυχή.

Thus speculations and postulations regarding the acausal only serve to obscure the nature of the acausal or distance us from that revealing of the acausal that empathy and πάθει μάθος and an appreciation of the numinous provide.

ἀρετή

Arête is the prized Hellenic virtue which can roughly be translated by the English word 'excellence' but which also implies what is naturally distinguishable - what is pre-eminent - because it reveals or shows certain valued qualities such as beauty, honour, valour, harmony.

Aristotelian Essentials

The essentials which Aristotle enumerated are: (i) Reality (existence) exists independently of us and our consciousness, and thus independent of our senses; (ii) our limited understanding of this independent 'external world' depends for the most part upon our senses, our faculties – that is, on what we can see, hear or touch; on what we can observe or come to know via our senses; (iii) logical argument, or reason, is perhaps the most important means to knowledge and understanding of and about this 'external world'; (iv) the cosmos (existence) is, of itself, a reasoned order subject to rational laws.

In addition such essentials now include Isaac Newton's first *Rules of Reasoning* which is that

> "We are to admit no more causes of natural things than such as are both true and sufficient to explain their appearances. To this purpose the philosophers say that Nature does nothing in vain, and more is in vain when less will serve; for Nature is pleased with simplicity, and affects not the pomp of superfluous causes."

Hence why it is often considered that there are five Aristotelian Essentials

Experimental science seeks to explain the natural world – the phenomenal world – by means of direct, personal observation of it, and by making deductions, and formulating hypothesis, based on such direct observation.

The philosophy of pathei-mathos adds the faculty of empathy - and the knowing so provided by empathy - to these essentials. Part of the knowing that empathy reveals, or can reveal, concerns the nature of Being, of beings, and of Time.

ἁρμονίη

ἁρμονίη (harmony) is or can be manifest/discovered by an individual cultivating wu-wei and σωφρονεῖν (a fair and balanced personal, individual, judgement).

Compassion

The English word compassion dates from around 1340 CE and the word in its original sense (and as used in this work) means benignity, which word derives from the Latin benignitatem, the sense imputed being of a kind, compassionate, well-mannered character, disposition, or deed. Benignity came into English usage around the same time as compassion; for example, the word occurs in Chaucer's Troilus and Criseyde [ii. 483] written around 1374 CE.

Hence, compassion is understood as meaning being kindly disposed toward and/or feeling a sympathy with someone (or some living being) affected by pain/suffering/grief or who is enduring vicissitudes.

The word compassion itself is derived from com, meaning together-with, combined with pati, meaning to-suffer/to-endure and derived from the classical Latin passiō. Thus useful synonyms for compassion, in this original sense, are compassivity and benignity.

Cosmic Perspective

The Cosmic Perspective refers to our place in the Cosmos, to the fact that we human beings are simply one fragile fallible mortal biological life-form on one planet orbiting one star in one galaxy in a Cosmos of billions of galaxies. Thus in terms of this perspective all our theories, our ideas, our beliefs, our abstractions are merely the opinionated product of our limited fallible Earth-bound so-called 'intelligence', an 'intelligence', an understanding, we foolishly, arrogantly, pridefully have a tendency to believe in and exalt as if we are somehow 'the centre of the Universe' and cosmically important.

The Cosmic Perspective inclines us – or can incline us – toward wu-wei, toward avoiding the error of hubris, toward humility, and thus toward an appreciation of the numinous.

δαίμων

A δαίμων is not one of the pantheon of major Greek gods – θεοί - but rather a lesser type of divinity who might be assigned by those gods to bring good fortune or misfortune to human beings and/or watch over certain human beings and especially particular numinous (sacred) places.

Denotatum

The term denotatum - from the Latin, denotare - is used in accord with its general meaning which is "to denote or to describe by an expression or a word; to name some-thing; to refer that which is so named or so denoted."

Thus understood, and used as an Anglicized term, denotatum is applicable to both singular and plural instances and thus obviates the need to employ the Latin plural denotata.

Descriptor

A descriptor is a word, a term, used to describe some-thing which exists and which is personally observed, or is discovered, by means of our senses (including the faculty of empathy).

A descriptor differs from an ideation, category, or abstraction, in that a descriptor describes what-is as 'it' is observed, according to its physis (its nature) whereas an abstraction, for example, denotes what is presumed/assumed/idealized, past or present or future. A descriptor relies on, is derived from, describes, individual knowing and individual judgement; an abstraction relies on something abstract, impersonal, such as some opinion/knowing/judgement of others or some assumptions, theory, or hypothesis made by others.

An example of a descriptor is the term 'violent' [using physical force sufficient to cause bodily harm or injury to a person or persons] to describe the observed behaviour of an individual. Another example would be the term 'extremist' to describe - to denote - a person who treats or who has been observed to treat others harshly/violently in pursuit of some supra-personal objective of a political or of a religious nature.

δίκη

Depending on context, δίκη could be the judgement of an individual (or Judgement personified), or the natural and the necessary balance, or the correct/customary/ancestral way, or what is expected due to custom, or what is considered correct and natural, and so on.

A personified Judgement - the Δίκην of Hesiod - is the goddess of the natural balance, evident in the ancestral customs, the ways, the way of life, the ethos, of a community, whose judgement, δίκη, is "in accord with", has the nature or the character of, what tends to restore such balance after some deed or deeds by an individual or individuals have upset or disrupted that balance. This sense of δίκη as one's ancestral customs is evident, for example, in Homer (Odyssey, III, 244).

In the philosophy of pathei-mathos, the term Δίκα - spelt thus in a modern way with a capital Δ - is sometimes used to intimate a new, a particular and numinous, philosophical principle, and differentiate Δίκα from the more general δίκη. As a numinous principle, or axiom, Δίκα thus suggests what lies beyond and what was the genesis of δίκη personified as the goddess, Judgement – the goddess of natural balance, of the ancestral way and ancestral customs.

Empathy

Etymologically, this fairly recent English word, used to translate the German Einfühlung, derives, via the late Latin sympathia, from the Greek συμπάθεια - συμπαθής - and is thus formed from the prefix σύν (sym) together with παθ- [root of πάθος] meaning enduring/suffering, feeling: πάσχειν, to endure/suffer.

As used and defined by the philosophy of pathei-mathos, empathy - ἐμπάθεια - is a natural human faculty: that is, a noble intuition about (a revealing of) another human being or another living being. When empathy is developed and used, as envisaged by that way of life, then it is a specific and extended type of συμπάθεια. That is, it is a type of and a means to knowing and understanding another human being and/or other living beings - and thus differs in nature from compassion.

Empathic knowing is different from, but supplementary and complimentary to, that knowing which may be acquired by means of the Aristotelian essentials of conventional philosophy and experimental science.

Empathy reveals or can reveal the nature, the ontology (the physis) - sans abstractions/ideations/words - of Being, of beings, and of Time. This revealing is of the the a-causal nature of Being, and of how beings have their genesis in the separation-of-otherness; and thus how we human beings are but causal, mortal, fallible, microcosmic emanations of ψυχή.

Enantiodromia

The unusual compound Greek word ἐναντιοδρομίας occurs in a summary of the philosophy of Heraclitus by Diogenes Laërtius.

Enantiodromia is the term used, in the philosophy of pathei-mathos, to describe the revealing, the process, of perceiving, feeling, knowing, beyond causal appearance and the separation-of-otherness, and thus when what has become separated – or has been incorrectly perceived as separated – returns to the wholeness, the unity, from whence it came forth. When, that is, beings are understood in their correct relation to Being, beyond the causal abstraction of different/conflicting ideated opposites, and when as a result, a reformation of the individual, occurs. A relation, an appreciation of the numinous, that empathy and pathei-mathos provide, and which relation and which appreciation the accumulated pathei-mathos of individuals over millennia have made us aware of or tried to inform us or teach us about.

An important and a necessary part of enantiodromia involves a discovery, a knowing, an acceptance, and - as prelude - an interior balancing within individuals, of what has hitherto been perceived and designated as the apparent opposites described by terms (descriptors) such as 'muliebral' and 'masculous'.

The balance attained by - which is - enantiodromia is that of simply feeling, accepting, discovering, the empathic, the human, the personal, scale of things and thus understanding our own fallibility-of-knowing, our limitations as a human being

ἔρις

Strife; discord; disruption; a quarrel between friends or kin. As in the Odyssey:

ἥ τ᾽ ἔριν Ἀτρεΐδησι μετ᾽ ἀμφοτέροισιν ἔθηκε.

Who placed strife between those two sons of Atreus

Odyssey, 3, 136

According to the recounted tales of Greek mythology attributed to Aesop, ἔρις was caused by, or was a consequence of, the marriage between a personified πόλεμος (as the δαίμων of kindred strife) and a personified ὕβρις (as the δαίμων of arrogant pride) with Polemos rather forlornly following Hubris around rather than vice versa. Eris is thus the child of Polemos and Hubris.

Extremism

By extreme is meant to be harsh, so that an extremist is a person who tends toward harshness, or who is harsh, or who supports/incites harshness, in pursuit of some objective, usually of a political or a religious nature. Here, harsh is: rough, severe, a tendency to be unfeeling, unempathic.

Hence extremism is considered to be: (a) the result of such harshness, and (b) the principles, the causes, the characteristics, that promote, incite, or describe the harsh action of extremists. In addition, a fanatic is considered to be someone with a surfeit of zeal or whose enthusiasm for some objective, or for some cause, is intemperate.

In the terms of the philosophy/way of pathei-mathos, an extremist is someone who commits the error of hubris; and error which enantiodromia - following from πάθει μάθος - can sometimes correct or forestall. The genesis of extremism - be such extremism personal, or described as political or religious - is when the separation-of-otherness is used as a means of personal and collective identity and pride, with some 'others' - or 'the others' - assigned to a category considered less worthy than the category we assign ourselves and 'our kind/type' to.

Extremist ideologies manifest an unbalanced, an excessive, masculous nature.

εὐταξία

The quality, the virtue, of self-restraint, of a balanced, well-mannered conduct especially under adversity or duress, of which Cicero wrote:

> Haec autem scientia continentur ea, quam Graeci εὐταξίαν nominant, non hanc, quam interpretamur modestiam, quo in verbo modus inest, sed illa est εὐταξία, in qua intellegitur ordinis conservatio
>
> Those two qualities are evident in that way described by the Greeks as εὐταξίαν although what is meant by εὐταξία is not what we mean by the moderation of the moderate, but rather what we consider is restrained behaviour...   [My translation]
>
> De Officiis, Liber Primus, 142

Honour

The English word honour dates from around 1200 CE, deriving from the Latin honorem (meaning refined, grace, beauty) via the Old French (and thence Anglo-Norman) onor/onur. As used by The Way of Pathei-Mathos, honour means an instinct for and an adherence to what is fair, dignified, and valourous. An honourable person is thus someone of manners, fairness, natural dignity, and valour.

In respect of early usage of the term, two quotes may be of interest. The first, from c. 1393 CE, is taken from a poem, in Middle English, by John Gower:

> And riht in such a maner wise
> Sche bad thei scholde hire don servise,
> So that Achilles underfongeth
> As to a yong ladi belongeth
> Honour, servise and reverence.

John Gower, Confessio Amantis. Liber Quintus vv. 2997-3001 [Macaulay, G.C., ed. The Works of John Gower. Oxford: Clarendon Press. 1901]

The second is from several centuries later:

" Honour - as something distinct from mere probity, and which supposes in gentlemen a stronger abhorrence of perfidy, falsehood, or cowardice, and a more elevated and delicate sense of the dignity of virtue, than are usually found in vulgar minds."

George Lyttelton. History of the Life of Henry the Second. London, Printed for J. Dodsley. M DCC LXXV II [1777] (A new ed., cor.) vol 3, p.178

In the philosophy of pathei-mathos, the personal virtue of honour is considered to be a presencing, a grounding, an expression, of ψυχή - of Life, of our φύσις - occurring when the insight (the knowing) of a developed empathy inclines us toward a compassion that is, of necessity, balanced by σωφρονεῖν and in accord with δίκη. That is, as a means to live, to behave, as empathy intimates we can or should in order to avoid committing the folly, the error, of ὕβρις, in order not to cause suffering, and in order to re-present, to acquire, ἁρμονίη.

Humility

Humility is used, in a spiritual context, to refer to that gentleness, that modest demeanour, that understanding, which derives from an appreciation of the numinous and also from one's own admitted uncertainty of knowing and one's acknowledgement of past mistakes. An uncertainty of knowing, an acknowledgement of mistakes, that often derive from πάθει μάθος.

Humility is thus the natural human balance that offsets the unbalance of hubris (ὕβρις) - the balance that offsets the unbalance of pride and arrogance, and the balance that offsets the unbalance of that certainty of knowing which is one basis for extremism, for extremist beliefs, for fanaticism and intolerance. That is, humility is a manifestation of the natural balance of Life; a restoration of ἁρμονίη, of δίκη, of σωφρονεῖν - of those qualities and virtues - that hubris and extremism, that ἔρις and πόλεμος, undermine, distance us from, and replace.

Ideation

To posit or to construct an ideated form - an assumed perfect (ideal) form or category or abstraction - of some-thing, based on the belief or the assumption that what is observed by the senses, or revealed by observation, is either an 'imperfect copy' or an approximation of that thing, which the additional assumption that such an ideated form contains or in some way expresses (or can express) 'the essence' or 'the ethos' of that thing and of similar things.

Ideation also implies that the ideated form is or can be or should be contrasted with what it considered or assumed to be its 'opposite'.

Immediacy-of-the-Moment

The term the 'immediacy-of-the-moment' describes both (i) the nature and the extent of the acausal knowing that empathy and pathei-mathos provide, and (ii) the nature and extent of the morality of the philosophy of pathei-mathos.

Empathy, for example, being a natural and an individual faculty, is limited in range and application, just as our faculties of sight and hearing are limited in range and application. These limits extend to only what is direct, immediate, and involve personal interactions with other humans or with other living beings. There is therefore, for the philosophy of pathei-mathos, an 'empathic scale of things' and an acceptance of our limitations of personal knowing and personal understanding. An acceptance of (i) the unwisdom, the hubris, of arrogantly making assumptions about who and what are beyond the range of our empathy and outside of our personal experience/beyond the scope of our pathei-mathos.

Morality, for the philosophy of pathei-mathos, is a result of individuals using the faculty of empathy; a consequence of the insight and the understanding (the acausal knowing) that empathy provides for individuals in the immediacy-of-the-moment. Thus, morality is considered to reside not in some abstract theory or some moralistic schemata presented in some written text which individuals have to accept and try and conform or aspire to, but rather in personal virtues - such as such as compassion and fairness, and εὐταξία - that arise or which can arise naturally through empathy, πάθει μάθος, and thus from an awareness and appreciation of the numinous.

Innocence

Innocence is regarded as an attribute of those who, being personally unknown to us, are therefore unjudged us by and who thus are given the benefit of the doubt. For this presumption of innocence of others – until direct personal experience, and individual and empathic knowing of them, prove otherwise – is the fair, the reasoned, the numinous, the human, thing to do.

Empathy and πάθει μάθος incline us toward treating other human beings as we ourselves would wish to be treated; that is they incline us toward fairness, toward self-restraint, toward being well-mannered, and toward an appreciation and understanding of innocence.

Masculous

Masculous is a term, a descriptor, used to refer to certain traits, abilities, and qualities that are conventionally and historically associated with men, such as competitiveness, aggression, a certain harshness, the desire to organize/control, and a desire for adventure and/or for conflict/war/violence/competition over and above personal love and culture. Extremist ideologies manifest an unbalanced, an excessive, masculous nature.

Masculous is from the Latin masculus and occurs, for example, in some seventeenth century works such as one by William Struther: "This is not only the language of Canaan, but also the masculous Schiboleth." *True Happines, or, King Davids Choice: Begunne In Sermons, And Now Digested Into A Treatise.* Edinbvrgh, 1633

Muliebral

The term muliebral derives from the classical Latin word muliebris, and in the context the philosophy of Pathei-Mathos refers to those positive traits, abilities, and qualities that are conventionally and historically associated with women, such as empathy, sensitivity, gentleness, compassion, and a desire to love and be loved over and above a desire for conflict/adventure/war.

Numinous

The numinous is what manifests or can manifest or remind us of (what can reveal) the natural balance of ψυχή; a balance which ὕβρις upsets. This natural balance - our being as human beings - is or can be manifest to us in or by what is harmonious, or what reminds us of what is harmonious and beautiful. In a practical way, it is what predisposes us not to commit ὕβρις, and thus what we regard or come to appreciate as 'sacred' and dignified; what expresses our developed humanity and thus places us, as individuals, in our correct relation to ψυχή, and which relation is that we are but one mortal emanation of ψυχή.

See Appendix II - From Mythoi To Empathy: A New Appreciation Of The Numinous - for more details.

Pathei-Mathos

The Greek term πάθει μάθος derives from The Agamemnon of Aeschylus (written c. 458 BCE), and can be interpreted, or translated, as meaning learning from adversary, or wisdom arises from (personal) suffering; or personal experience is the genesis of true learning.

When understood in its Aeschylean context, it implies that for we human beings pathei-mathos possesses a numinous, a living, authority. That is, the understanding that arises from one's own personal experience - from formative experiences that involve some hardship, some grief, some personal suffering - is often or could be more valuable to us (more alive, more relevant, more meaningful) than any doctrine, than any religious faith, than any words/advice one might hear from someone else or read in some book.

Thus, pathei-mathos, like empathy, offers we human beings a certain conscious understanding, a knowing; and, when combined, pathei-mathos and empathy are or can be a guide to wisdom, to a particular conscious knowledge concerning our own nature (our physis), our relation to Nature, and our relation to other human beings, leading to an appreciation of the numinous and an appreciation of virtues such as humility and εὐταξία.

Politics

By the term politics is meant both of the following, according to context. (i) The theory and practice of governance, with governance itself founded on two fundamental assumptions; that of some minority - a government (elected or unelected), some military authority, some oligarchy, some ruling elite, some tyrannos, or some leader - having or assuming authority (and thus power and influence) over others, and with that authority being exercised over a specific geographic area or territory. (ii) The activities of those individuals or groups whose aim or whose intent is to obtain and exercise some authority or some control over - or to influence - a society or sections of a society by means which are organized and directed toward changing/reforming that society or sections of a society in accordance with a particular ideology.

Πόλεμος

Heraclitus fragment 80

Πόλεμος is not some abstract 'war' or strife or kampf, but rather that which is or becomes the genesis of beings from Being (the separation of beings from Being), and thus not only that which manifests as δίκη but also accompanies ἔρις because it is the nature of Πόλεμος that beings, born because of and by ἔρις, can be returned to Being, become bound together - be whole - again by enantiodromia.

According to the recounted tales of Greek mythology attributed to Aesop, ἔρις was caused by, or was a consequence of, the marriage between a personified πόλεμος (as the δαίμων of kindred strife) and a personified ὕβρις (as the δαίμων of arrogant pride) with Polemos rather forlornly following Hubris around rather than vice versa. Thus Eris is the child of Polemos and Hubris.

Furthermore, Polemos was originally the δαίμων (not the god) of kindred strife, whether familial, of friends, or of one's πόλις (one's clan and their places of dwelling). Thus, to describe Polemos, as is sometimes done, as the god of war, is doubly incorrect.

Physis (φύσις)

See Appendix IV: The Concept Of Physis.

Religion

By religion is meant organized worship, devotion, and faith, where there is: (i) a belief in some deity/deities, or in some supreme Being or in some supra-personal power who/which can reward or punish the individual, and (ii) a distinction made between the realm of the sacred/the-gods/God/the-revered and the realm of the ordinary or the human.

The term organized here implies an established institution, body or group - or a plurality of these - who or which has at least to some degree codified the faith and/or the acts of worship and devotion, and which is accepted as having some authority or has established some authority among the adherents. This codification can relate to accepting as authoritative certain writings and/or a certain book or books.

Separation-of-Otherness

The separation-of-otherness is a term used to describe the implied or assumed causal separateness of living beings, a part of which is the distinction we make (instinctive or otherwise) between our self and the others. Another part is assigning our self, and the-others, to (or describing them and us by) some category/categories, and to which category/categories we ascribe (or to which category/categories has/have been ascribed) certain qualities or attributes.

Given that a part of such ascription/denoting is an assumption or assumptions of worth/value/difference and of inclusion/exclusion, the separation-of-otherness is the genesis of hubris; causes and perpetuates conflict and suffering; and is a path away from ἁρμονίη, δίκη, and thus from wisdom.

The separation-of-otherness conceals the nature of Beings and beings; a nature which empathy and pathei-mathos can reveal.

Society

By the term society is meant a collection of people who live in a specific geographic area or areas and whose association or interaction is mostly determined by a shared set of guidelines or principles or beliefs, irrespective of whether these are written or unwritten, and irrespective of whether such guidelines/principles/beliefs are willingly accepted or accepted on the basis of acquiescence. These shared guidelines or principles or beliefs often tend to form an ethos and a culture and become the basis for what is considered moral (and good) and thence become the inspiration for laws and/or constitutions.

As used here, the term refers to 'modern societies' (especially those of the modern West).

σωφρονεῖν

I use σωφρονεῖν (sophronein) in preference to σωφροσύνη (sophrosyne) since sophrosyne has acquired an English interpretation – "soundness of mind, moderation" – which in my view distorts the meaning of the original Greek. As with my use of the term πάθει μάθος (pathei-mathos) I use σωφρονεῖν in an Anglicized manner with there thus being no necessity to employ inflective forms.

State

By the term The State is meant:

The concept of both (1) organizing and controlling – over a particular and large geographical area – land (and resources); and (2) organizing and controlling individuals over that same geographical particular and large geographical area by: (a) the use of physical force or the threat of force and/or by influencing or persuading or manipulating a sufficient number of people to accept some leader/clique/minority/representatives as the legitimate authority; (b) by means of the central administration and centralization of resources (especially fiscal and military); and (c) by the mandatory taxation of personal income.

The Good

For the philosophy of Pathei-Mathos, 'the good' is considered to be what is fair; what alleviates or does not cause suffering; what is compassionate; what is honourable; what is reasoned and balanced. This knowing of the good arises from the (currently underused and undeveloped) natural human faculty of empathy, and which empathic knowing is different from, supplementary and complimentary to, that knowing which may be acquired by means of the Aristotelian essentials of conventional philosophy and experimental science.

Time

In the philosophy of pathei-mathos, Time is considered to be an expression of the nature - the φύσις - of beings, and thus, for living beings, is a variable emanation of ψυχή, differing from being to being, and representing how that living being can change (is a fluxion) or may change or has changed, which such change (such fluxions) being a-causal.

Time - as conventionally understood and as measured/represented by a terran-calendar with durations marked days, weeks, and years - is therefore regarded as an abstraction, and an abstraction which tends to conceal the nature of living beings.

ὕβρις

ὕβρις (hubris) is the error of personal insolence, of going beyond the proper limits set by: (a) reasoned (balanced) judgement – σωφρονεῖν – and by (b) an awareness, a personal knowing, of the numinous, and which knowing of the numinous can arise from empathy and πάθει μάθος.

Hubris upsets the natural balance – is contrary to ἁρμονίη [harmony] – and often results from a person or persons striving for or clinging to some causal abstraction.

According to The Way of Pathei-Mathos, ὕβρις disrupts - and conceals - our appreciation of what is numinous and thus of what/whom we should respect, classically understood as ψυχή and θεοί and Μοῖραι τρίμορφοι μνήμονές τ᾽ Ἐρινύες and δαιμόνων and those sacred places guarded or watched over by δαιμόνων.

Way

The philosophy of pathei-mathos makes a distinction between a religion and a spiritual Way of Life. One of the differences being that a religion requires and manifests a codified ritual and doctrine and a certain expectation of conformity in terms of doctrine and ritual, as well as a certain organization beyond the local community level resulting in particular individuals assuming or being appointed to positions of authority in matters relating to that religion. In contrast, Ways are more diverse and more an expression of a spiritual ethos, of a customary, and often localized, way of doing certain spiritual things, with there generally being little or no organization beyond the community level and no individuals assuming - or being appointed by some organization - to positions of authority in matters relating to that ethos.

Religions thus tend to develope an organized regulatory and supra-local hierarchy which oversees and appoints those, such as priests or religious teachers, regarded as proficient in spiritual matters and in matters of doctrine and ritual, whereas adherents of Ways tend to locally and informally and communally, and out of respect and a personal knowing, accept certain individuals as having a detailed knowledge and an understanding of the ethos and the practices of that Way.

Many spiritual Ways have evolved into religions.

Wisdom

Wisdom is both the ability of reasoned - a balanced - judgement, σωφρονεῖν, a discernment; and a particular conscious knowledge concerning our own nature, and our relation to Nature, to other life and other human beings: rerum divinarum et humanarum. Part of this knowledge is of how we human beings are often balanced between honour and dishonour; balanced between ὕβρις and ἀρετή; between our animalistic desires, our passions, and our human ability to be noble, to morally develope ourselves; a balance manifest in our known ability to be able to control, to restrain, ourselves, and thus find and follow a middle way, of ἁρμονίη.

Wu-wei

Wu-wei is a Taoist term used in The Way of Pathei-Mathos/The Numinous Way to refer to a personal 'letting-be' deriving from a feeling, a knowing, that an essential part of wisdom is cultivation of an interior personal balance and which cultivation requires acceptance that one must work with, or employ, things according to their nature, their φύσις, for to do otherwise is incorrect, and inclines us toward, or is, being excessive – that is, toward the error, the unbalance, that is hubris, an error often manifest in personal arrogance, excessive personal pride, and insolence - that is, a disrespect for the numinous.

In practice, the knowledge, the understanding, the intuition, the insight that is wu-wei is a knowledge, an understanding, that can be acquired from empathy, πάθει μάθος, and by a knowing of and an appreciation of the numinous. This knowledge and understanding is of wholeness, and that life, things/beings, change, flow, exist, in certain natural ways which we human beings cannot change however hard we might try; that such a hardness of human trying, a belief in such hardness, is unwise, un-natural, upsets the natural balance and can cause misfortune/suffering for us and/or for others, now or in the future. Thus success lies in discovering the inner nature (the physis) of things/beings /ourselves and gently, naturally, slowly, working with this inner nature, not striving against it.

ψυχή

Life qua being. Our being as a living existent is considered an emanation of ψυχή. Thus ψυχή is what 'animates' us and what gives us our nature, φύσις, as human beings. Our nature is that of a mortal fallible being veering between σωφρονεῖν (thoughtful reasoning, and thus fairness) and ὕβρις.

Footnotes

[1]

Ζῆνα δέ τις προφρόνως ἐπινίκια κλάζων
τεύξεται φρενῶν τὸ πᾶν:
ὸν φρονεῖν βροτοὺς ὁδώ-
σαντα, τὸν πάθει μάθος
θέντα κυρίως ἔχειν.

    If anyone, from reasoning, exclaims loudly that victory of Zeus,
    Then they have acquired an understanding of all these things;
    Of he who guided mortals to reason,
    Who laid down that this possesses authority:
    Learning from adversity.

Aeschylus: Agamemnon,174-183

[2] An awareness of the numinous is what predisposes us not to commit the error, the folly, of ὕβρις. As Sophocles wrote in Oedipus Tyrannus:

    ὕβρις φυτεύει τύραννον:
    ὕβρις, εἰ πολλῶν ὑπερπλησθῆ μάταν,
    ἃ μὴ ʼπίκαιρα μηδὲ συμφέροντα,
    ἀκρότατον εἰσαναβᾶσʼ
    αἶπος ἀπότομον ὤρουσεν εἰς ἀνάγκαν,
    ἔνθʼ οὐ ποδὶ χρησίμῳ
    χρῆται

    Insolence plants the tyrant. There is insolence if by a great foolishness
    there is a useless over-filling which goes beyond the proper limits. It
    is an ascending to the steepest and utmost heights and then that
    hurtling toward that Destiny where the useful foot has no use...
    (vv.872ff)

In respect of the numinous, basically it is what manifests or can manifest or remind us of (what can reveal) the natural balance of ψυχή; a balance which ὕβρις upsets. This natural balance - our being as human beings - is or can be manifest to us in or by what is harmonious, or what reminds us of what is harmonious and beautiful. In a practical way, it is what we regard or come to appreciate as 'sacred' and dignified; what expresses our humanity and thus places us, as individuals, in our correct relation to ψυχή, and which relation is that we are but one mortal emanation of ψυχή.

We are reminded of this natural balance, of what is numinous - we can come to know, to experience, the numinous and thus can understand the nature of our being - by πάθει μάθος and empathy. That is, by the process of learning from personal adversity/personal suffering/personal grief and by using and developing our faculty of empathy.

An aspect of this learning is an appreciation, an awareness, of the Cosmic Perspective: of ourselves as one fallible, mortal, fragile biological, microcosmic, nexion on one planet in one Galaxy in a Cosmos of billions of galaxies; one connexion to, one emanation of, all other Life. In essence, πάθει μάθος and empathy teach us or can teach us humility, compassion, and the importance of personal love.

[3] The essentials which Aristotle enumerated are: (i) Reality (existence) exists independently of us and our consciousness, and thus independent of our senses; (ii) our limited understanding of this independent 'external world' depends for the most part upon our senses - that is, on what we can see, hear or touch; that is, on what we can observe or come to know via our senses; (iii) logical argument, or reason, is perhaps the most important means to knowledge and understanding of and about this 'external world'; (iv) the cosmos (existence) is, of itself, a reasoned order subject to rational laws.

Experimental science seeks to explain the natural world – the phenomenal world – by means of direct, personal observation of it, and by making deductions, and formulating hypothesis, based on such direct observation, with the important and necessary proviso, expressed by Isaac Newton in his Principia, that

> "We are to admit no more causes of natural things than such as are both true and sufficient to explain their appearance..... for Nature is pleased with simplicity, and affects not the pomp of superfluous causes."

[4] The sense of τύραννος is not exactly what our fairly modern term tyrant is commonly regarded as imputing. Rather, it refers to the intemperate person of excess who is so subsumed with some passion or some aim or a lust for power that they go far beyond the due, the accepted, bounds of behaviour and thus exceed the limits of or misuse whatever authority they have been entrusted with. Thus do they, by their excess, by their disrespect for the customs of their ancestors, by their lack of reasoned, well-balanced, judgement [σωφρονεῖν] offend the gods, and thus, to restore the balance, do the Ἐρινύες take revenge. For it is in the nature of the τύραννος that they forget, or they scorn, the truth, the ancient wisdom, that their lives are subject to, guided by, Μοῖραι τρίμορφοι μνήμονές τ᾽ Ἐρινύες -

τίς οὖν ἀνάγκης ἐστὶν οἰακοστρόφος.

Μοῖραι τρίμορφοι μνήμονές τ᾽ Ἐρινύες

Who then compels to steer us?
Trimorphed Moirai with their ever-heedful Furies!

Aeschylus (attributed), Prometheus Bound, 515-6

[5] Heraclitus, fragment 80:

εἰδέναι δὲ χρὴ τὸν πόλεμον ἐόντα ξυνόν, καὶ δίκην ἔριν, καὶ γινόμενα πάντα κατ᾽ ἔριν καὶ χρεώμενα [χρεών]

One should be aware that Polemos pervades, with discord δίκη, and that beings are naturally born by discord.

See my Heraclitus - Some Translations and Notes. (Fifth Edition, 2012)

In respect of the modern error of ὕβρις that is extremism, an error manifest in extremists, my understanding of an extremist is a person who tends toward harshness, or who is harsh, or who supports/incites harshness, in pursuit of some objective, usually of a political or a religious. See Appendix VII.

[6] See The Change of Enantiodromia.

[7] The meaning here of ψυχή is derived from the usage of Homer, Aeschylus, Aristotle, etcetera, and implies Life qua being. Or, expressed another way, living beings are emanations of, and thus manifest, ψυχή. This sense of ψυχή is beautifully expressed in a, in my view, rather mis-understood fragment attributed to Heraclitus:

ψυχῆισιν θάνατος ὕδωρ γενέσθαι, ὕδατι δὲ θάνατος γῆν γενέσθαι, ἐκ γῆς δὲ ὕδωρ γίνεται, ἐξ ὕδατος δὲ ψυχή. Fragment 36

Where the water begins our living ends and where earth begins water ends, and yet earth nurtures water and from that water, Life.

[8] In respect of the numinous principle of Δίκα, refer to Appendix I - The Principle of Δίκα.

[9] Although φύσις has a natural tendency to become covered up (Φύσις κρύπτεσθαι φιλεῖ - concealment accompanies Physis) it can be uncovered through λόγος and πάθει μάθος.

[10] Wu-wei is a Taoist term used in The Way of Pathei-Mathos to refer to a personal 'letting-be' deriving from a feeling, a knowing, that an essential part of wisdom is cultivation of an interior personal balance and which cultivation requires acceptance that one must work with, or employ, things according to their nature, their φύσις, for to do otherwise is incorrect, and inclines us toward, or is, being excessive – that is, toward the error, the unbalance, that is hubris, an error often manifest in personal arrogance, excessive personal pride, and insolence - that is, a disrespect for the numinous.

In practice, the knowledge, the understanding, the intuition, the insight that is wu-wei is a knowledge, an understanding, that can be acquired from empathy, πάθει μάθος, and by a knowing of and an appreciation of the numinous. This knowledge and understanding is of wholeness and that life, things/beings, change, flow, exist, in certain natural ways which we human beings cannot change however hard we might try; that such a hardness of human trying, a belief in such hardness, is unwise, un-natural, upsets the natural balance and can cause misfortune/suffering for us and/or for others, now or in the future. Thus success lies in discovering the inner nature (the physis) of things/beings /ourselves and gently, naturally, slowly, working with this inner nature, not striving against it.

[11] Heraclitus, fragment 112:

> σωφρονεῖν ἀρετὴ μεγίστη, καὶ σοφίη ἀληθέα λέγειν καὶ ποιεῖν κατὰ φύσιν ἐπαίοντας

> Most excellent is balanced reasoning, for that skill can tell inner character from outer.

[12] In particular, The Agamemnon of Aeschylus; and the Oedipus Tyrannus, and Antigone, of Sophocles. In respect of Oedipus Tyrannus, refer, for example, to vv.863ff and vv.1329-1338

In much mis-understood verses in The Agamemnon (1654-1656) Clytaemnestra makes it known that she still is aware of the power, and importance, of δίκη. Of not killing to excess:

> μηδαμῶς, ὦ φίλτατ᾽ ἀνδρῶν, ἄλλα δράσωμεν κακά.
> ἀλλὰ καὶ τάδ᾽ ἐξαμῆσαι πολλά, δύστηνον θέρος.
> πημονῆς δ᾽ ἅλις γ᾽ ὑπάρχει: μηδὲν αἱματώμεθα.

The aforementioned verses are often mis-translated to give some nonsense such as: 'No more violence. Here is a monstrous harvest and a bitter reaping time. There is pain enough already. Let us not be bloody now'.

However, what Aeschylus actually has Clytaemnestra say is:

> "Let us not do any more harm for to reap these many would make it an unlucky harvest: injure them just enough, but do not stain us with their blood."

She is being practical (and quite Hellenic) and does not want to bring misfortune (from the gods) upon herself, or Aegisthus, by killing to excess. The killings she has done are, however, quite acceptable to her - she has vigorously defended them claiming it was her natural duty to avenge her daughter and the insult done to her by Agamemnon bringing his mistress, Cassandra, into her home. Clytaemnestra shows no pity for the Elders whom Aegisthus wishes to kill: "if you must", she says, "you can injure them. But do not kill them - that would be unlucky for us." That would be going just too far, and overstep what she still perceives as the natural, the proper, limits of mortal behaviour.

[13] Two fragments attributed to Heraclitus are of interest in this respect - 112, and 123. Refer to my Heraclitus - Some Translations and Notes. (Fifth Edition, 2012)

[14] Hesiod, Theogony v. 901 - Εὐνουμίην τε Δίκην τε καὶ Εἰρήνην τεθαλυῖαν

In effect, a personified Judgement is the goddess of the natural balance - evident in the ancestral customs, the ways, the way of life, the ethos, of a community - whose judgement, δίκη, is "in accord with", has the nature or the character of, what tends to restore such balance after some deed or deeds by an individual or individuals have upset or disrupted that balance. This sense of δίκη as one's ancestral customs is evident, for example, in Homer's Odyssey:

> νῦν δ᾽ ἐθέλω ἔπος ἄλλο μεταλλῆσαι καὶ ἐρέσθαι
> Νέστορ᾽, ἐπεὶ περὶ οἶδε δίκας ἠδὲ φρόνιν ἄλλων
> τρὶς γὰρ δή μίν φασιν ἀνάξασθαι γένε᾽ ἀνδρῶν
> ὥς τέ μοι ἀθάνατος ἰνδάλλεται εἰσοράασθαι
>
> Book III, 243-246
>
> I now wish to ask Nestor some questions to find out about some other things,
> For he understands others and knows more about our customs than them,
> Having been - so it is said - a Chieftain for three generations of mortals,
> And, to look at, he seems to me to be one of those immortals

[15] Πόλεμος is not some abstract 'war' or strife or kampf, but rather that which is or becomes the genesis of beings from Being (the separation of beings from

Being), and thus not only that which manifests as δίκη but also accompanies ἔρις because it is the nature of Πόλεμος that beings, born because of and by ἔρις, can be returned to Being, become bound together - be whole - again by enantiodromia.

Thus πόλεμος - like ψυχή and πάθει μάθος and ἐναντιοδρομίας and ὕβρις and δίκη as δίκη/Δίκην/Δίκα - is a philosophical principle and should therefore in my view not be blandly translated by a single word or term, but rather should be left untranslated or be transliterated, thus requiring for its understanding a certain thoughtful reasoning and thence interpretation according to context.

In respect of such interpretation, it is for example interesting that in the recounted tales of Greek mythology attributed to Aesop, and in circulation at the time of Heraclitus, a personified πόλεμος (as the δαίμων of kindred strife) married a personified ὕβρις (as the δαίμων of arrogant pride) and that it was a common folk belief that πόλεμος accompanied ὕβρις - that is, that Polemos followed Hubris around rather than vice versa, causing or bringing ἔρις.

[16] See Appendix VII. The saying - attributed to Heraclitus - is from Diogenes Laërtius, Lives of Eminent Philosophers (ix. 7)

[17] Fragment 112.

[18] For an explanation is what is meant here by innocence, see the entry in Appendix VII.

[19] Part I: The Way of Pathei-Mathos - A Philosophical Compendiary

[20] To assess is to reasonably consider and thus arrive at a balanced, a reasonable, a fair, judgement/assessment.

[21] qv. 'An Appreciation of The Numinous' in The Way of Pathei-Mathos - A Philosophical Compendiary

[22] Fragments 53 and 80

[23] Fragment 52

[24] Fragment 64

[25] Fragment 123

[26] The State is defined in Appendix VI - A Glossary of Terms.

As mentioned elsewhere, I am somewhat idiosyncratic regarding capitalization (and spelling), and capitalize certain words, such as State, and often use terms such as The State to emphasize the philosophical truth of State as entity.

[27] The ethics of the way of pathei-mathos are the ethics of empathy - of συμπάθεια. In practical personal terms, this means dignity, fairness, balance (δίκη), reason, a lack of prejudgement, and the requirement of a personal knowing and of personal experience, of πάθει μάθος.

An ethical person thus reveals, possesses, εὐταξία - the quality, the personal virtue, of self-restraint; of personal orderly (balanced, honourable, well-mannered) conduct, a virtue especially evident under adversity or duress.

Thus, and as mentioned in Part Three - Enantiodromia and The Reformation of The Individual, the good is considered to be what is fair; what alleviates or does not cause suffering; what is compassionate; what empathy by its revealing inclines us to do, what inclines us to appreciate the numinous and why ὕβρις is an error of unbalance.

Hence the bad - what is wrong, immoral - is what is unfair; what is harsh and unfeeling; what intentionally causes or contributes to suffering, with what is bad often considered to be due to a lack of empathy and of πάθει μάθος in a person, and a consequence of a bad φύσις, of a bad, a rotten, or an undeveloped, unformed, not-mature, individual character/nature. In effect, such a bad person lacks εὐταξία, has little or no appreciation of the numinous, and is often in thrall to their hubriatic and/or their masculous desires.

[28] Heraclitus, fragment 80: εἰδέναι δὲ χρὴ τὸν πόλεμον ἐόντα ξυνόν, καὶ δίκην ἔριν, καὶ γινόμενα πάντα κατ᾽ ἔριν καὶ χρεώμενα [χρεών]

One should be aware that Polemos pervades, with discord δίκη, and that beings are naturally born by discord.

See my *Heraclitus - Some Translations and Notes*. (Fifth Edition, 2012)

[29] In respect of the numinous principle of Δίκα, refer to Appendix I.

[30] Although φύσις has a natural tendency to become covered up (Φύσις κρύπτεσθαι φιλεῖ - concealment accompanies Physis) it can be uncovered through λόγος and πάθει μάθος.

[31] I have used a transliteration of the compound Greek word - ἐναντιοδρομίας - rather than given a particular translation, since the term enantiodromia in my view suggests the uniqueness of expression of the original, and which original in my view is not adequately, and most certainly not accurately, described by a usual translation such as 'conflict of opposites'. Rather, what is suggested is 'confrontational contest' - that is, by facing up to the expected/planned /inevitable contest.

Interestingly, Carl Jung - who was familiar with the sayings of Heraclitus - used the term enantiodromia to describe the emergence of a trait (of character) to offset another trait and so restore a certain psychological balance within the individual.

[32] Refer to my *Heraclitus - Some Translations and Notes*. (Fifth Edition, 2012)

[33] While Φύσις (Physis) has a natural tendency to become covered up (Heraclitus, Fragment 123) it can be uncovered through λόγος and πάθει μάθος.

[34] In *Empathy and The Immoral Abstraction of Race*.

[35] Πόλεμος πάντων μὲν πατήρ ἐστι, πάντων δὲ βασιλεύς, καὶ τοὺς μὲν θεοὺς ἔδειξε τοὺς δὲ ἀνθρώπους, τοὺς μὲν δούλους ἐποίησε τοὺς δὲ ἐλευθέρους. Fragmentum 53.

[36] See my Heraclitus - Some Translations and Notes (Fifth Edition, 2012) where I suggest a new interpretation of Fragmentum 53: Polemos our genesis, governing us all to bring forth some gods, some mortal beings with some unfettered yet others kept bound.

[37] I have deliberately transliterated (instead of translated) polemos, and left δίκη as δίκη. In respect of δίκη, see Appendix VII - Glossary of Terms.

Alternative renderings of the fragment are:

a) One should be aware that polemos is pervasive; and discord δίκη, and that beings [our being] quite naturally come-into-being through discord

b) One should be aware that polemos pervades; with discord δίκη, and that all beings are begotten because of discord.

[38] Correctly understood, a δαίμων is not one of the pantheon of major Greek gods - θεοί - but rather a lesser type of divinity who might be assigned by those gods to bring good fortune or misfortune to human beings and/or watch over certain human beings and especially particular numinous (sacred) places.

In addition, Polemos was originally the δαίμων of kindred strife, whether familial, or of one's πόλις (one's clan and their places of dwelling). Thus, to describe Polemos, as is sometimes done, as the god of conflict (or war), is doubly incorrect.

It is interesting to observe how the term δαίμων - with and after Plato, and especially by its use by the early Christian Church - came to be a moral abstraction, used in a bad sense (as 'demon'), and contrasted with another moral abstraction, that of 'angels'. Indeed, this process - this change - with this particular term is a reasonable metaphor for what we may call the manufacture and development of abstractions, and in which development the ontology and theology of an organized monotheistic religion played a not insignificant part.

[39] Agamemnon,174-183. qv. *Pathei-Mathos as Authority and Way* in The Way of Pathei-Mathos.

[40] Aeschylus (attributed), Prometheus Bound, 515-6

[41] qv. *The Nature of Being and of Beings* in The Way of Pathei-Mathos.

[42] The numinous is what predisposes us not to commit ὕβρις – that is, what continues or maintains or manifests ἁρμονίη and thus καλλός; the natural balance – sans abstractions – that enables us to know and appreciate, and which uncovers, Φύσις

Made in the USA
Las Vegas, NV
08 October 2024

96423388R10052